THE BLIGHT OF ASIA

*An Account of the Systematic Extermination of Christian
Populations by Mohammedans and of the Culpability
of Certain Great Powers; with the True Story
of the Burning of Smyrna*

By

George Horton

For Thirty Years Consul and Consul-General
of the United States in the Near East

With a Foreword by

James W. Gerard

Former Ambassador to Germany

Sterndale Classics
London

The Blight of Asia was originally printed by Bobbs-Merrill Company in 1926. It is produced here as an original reprint which includes the silent editing of spelling errors, and the addition of an index of proper nouns. Sterndale Classics is committed to republishing books with fidelity to original materials.

Published by Taderon Press, PO Box 2735, Reading, RG4 8GF, England by arrangement with Sterndale Classics.

© 2003 Ara Sarafian. All Rights Reserved.

Printed in association with the Gomidas Institute.

07 06 05 04 03   5 4 3 2 1

ISBN 1 903656 15 X

For further comments please write to:
Sterndale Classics
PO Box 32665
London, W14 0XT
Email: books@sterndaleclassics.co.uk

Table of Contents

Illustrations

THE BLIGHT OF ASIA

"What thou seest, write in a book, and send it unto churches which are in Asia; unto Ephesus, and unto Smyrna, and unto Pergamos, and unto Thyatira, and unto Sardis, and unto Philadelphia, and unto Laodicea."

REVELATIONS, I:11

THE MARTYRED CITY

Glory and Queen of Island Sea
     Was Smyrna, the beautiful city,
And fairest pearl of the Orient she—
     O Smyrna the beautiful city!
Heiress of countless storied ages,
Mother of poets, saints and sages,
     Was Smyrna, the beautiful city!

One of the ancient, glorious Seven
     Was Smyrna, the sacred city,
Whose candles all were alight in Heaven—
     O Smyrna the sacred city!
One of the Seven hopes and desires,
One of the seven Holy Fires
     Was Smyrna, the Sacred City.

And six fared out in the long ago-
     O Smyrna, the Christian city!
But hers shone on with a constant glow—
     O Smyrna, the Christian city!
The others died down and passed away,
But hers gleamed on until yesterday—
     O Smyrna, the Christian city!

Silent and dead are churchbell ringers
     Of Smyrna, the Christian city,
The music silent and dead the singers
     Of Smyrna, the happy city;
And her maidens, pearls of the Island seas
Are gone from the marble palaces
     Of Smyrna, enchanting city!

She is dead and rots by the Orient's gate,
    Does Smyrna, the murdered city,
Her artisans gone, her streets desolate—
    O Smyrna, the murdered city!
Her children made orphans, widows her wives
While under her stones the foul rat thrives—
    O Smyrna, the murdered city!

They crowned with a halo her bishop there,
    In Smyrna, the martyred city,
Though dabbled with blood was his long white hair—
    O Smyrna, the martyred city!
So she kept the faith in Christendom
From Polycarp to St. Chrysostom,[*]
    Did Smyrna, the glorified city!

---

[*] Martyred at Smyrna, September 1922.

FOREWORD

HERE at last is the truth about the destruction of Smyrna and the massacre of a large part of its inhabitants by one who was present. The writer of the following pages is a man, happily, who is not restrained from telling what he knows by political reasons or by any consideration of fear or self-interest. He gives the whole story of the savage extermination of Christian civilization throughout the length and breadth of the old Byzantine Empire in a clear and convincing manner.

That it should have been possible twenty centuries after the birth of Christ for a small and backward nation, like the Turks, to have committed such crimes against civilization and the progress of the world, is a matter which should cause all conscientious people to pause and think; yet the writer shows conclusively that these crimes have been committed without opposition on the part of any Christian nation and that the last frightful scene at Smyrna was enacted within a few yards of powerful Allied and American battle fleet.

We turned a deaf ear to the dying Christians, when they called to us for aid, fully aware that America was their only hope, and now it would appear that there is a growing tendency in this country to whitewash the Turks and condone their crimes in order to obtain material advantages from them.

The author takes the position that this can not be done, as the Turks have put so great an affront upon humanity that it can not easily be overlooked, and the truth is sure to come out. He claims that high ideals are more than oil or railroads, and that the Turks should not be accepted into the society of decent nations until they show sincere repentance for their crimes.

Fraternizing with them on any other terms creates a suspicion of sordidness or even complicity. From the outspoken nature of this book it will be evident to the reader that the writing of it has required considerable courage and that it has been inspired by no other possible motive than a desire to make the truth known about matters which it is important for the world to know.

(Signed) JAMES W. GERARD

Weeding Out the Men. All men of military age were torn away from their wives and children and led away in groups for deportation to the interior.

INTRODUCTION

THE editor of a great Paris journal once remarked that he attributed the extraordinary success of his publication to the fact that he had discovered that each man had at least one story to tell.

I have been for many years in the Near East—about thirty in all—and have watched the gradual and systematic extermination of Christians and Christianity in that region, and I believe it my duty to tell that grim tale, and to turn the light upon the political rivalries of the Western World, that have made such a fearful tragedy possible.

Though I have served for the major part of time as an American consular officer, I am no longer acting in that capacity, and have no further connection with the United States Government. None of the statements, which I make, therefore, has any official weight, nor have I in any way drawn upon State Department records or sources of information. I write strictly in my capacity as a private citizen, drawing my facts from my own observations, and from the testimony of others whom I quote.

I was in Athens in July, 1908, when, at the instigation of the Young Turks' "Committee of Union and Progress" the Saloniki army revolted and demanded the immediate putting into effect of the Constitution of 1876, which had become a dead letter, and I noted the reaction produced upon Greece by that apparently progressive move.

I was in Saloniki shortly after and witnessed the sad awakening of the non-Mussulman elements of that part of the Balkans to the fact that the much vaunted "Constitution" meant no liberty for them, but rather suppression, suffering and ultimate extinction.

I was in Smyrna in May of 1917, when Turkey severed relations with the United States, and I received the oral and written statements of native-born American eye-witnesses of the vast and incredibly horrible Armenian massacres of 1915–16—some of which will be here given for the first time; I personally observed and otherwise confirmed the outrageous treatment of the Christian population of the Smyrna vilayet, both during the Great War, and before its outbreak. I returned to Smyrna later and was there up until the evening of September 11, 1922, on which date the city was set on fire by the army of Mustapha Khemal, and a large part of its population done to death, and I witnessed the development of that Dantesque tragedy, which possesses few, if any parallels in the history of the world.

One object of writing this book is to make the truth known concerning these very significant events and to throw the light on an important period during which colossal crimes have been committed against the human race, with Christianity losing ground in Europe and America as well as in Africa and the Near East.

Another object is to give the church people of the United States the opportunity of deciding whether they wish to continue pouring millions of dollars, collected by contributions small and great, into Turkey for the purpose of supporting schools, which no longer permit the Bible to be read or Christ to be taught; whether, in fact, they are not doing more harm than good to the Christian cause and name, by sustaining institutions which have accepted such a compromise?

Another object is to show that the destruction of Smyrna was but the closing act in a consistent program of exterminating Christianity throughout the length and breadth of the old Byzantine Empire; the expatriation of an ancient Christian civilization, which in recent years had begun to take on growth and rejuvenation spiritually, largely as a result of the labors of American missionary teachers. Their admirable institutions, scattered all over Turkey, which have cost the people of the United States between fifty million and eighty million dollars, have been, with some exceptions, closed or irreparably damaged, and their thousands of Christian teachers and pupils butchered or dispersed. This process of extermination was carried on over a considerable period of time, with fixed purpose, with system, and with painstaking minute details; and it was accomplished with unspeakable cruelties, causing the destruction of a greater number of human beings than have suffered in any similar persecution since the coming of Christ.

I have been cognizant of what was going on for a number of years and when I came back to America after the Smyrna tragedy and saw the prosperous people crowded in their snug warm churches, I could hardly restrain myself from rising to my feet and shouting: "For every convert that you make here, a Christian throat is being cut over there; while your creed is losing ground in Europe and America,

Mohammed is forging ahead in Africa and the Near East with torch and scimitar."

Another reason is to call attention to the general hardening of human hearts that seems to have developed since the days of Gladstone—a less exalted and more shifty attitude of mind. This is partly due to the fact that men's sensibilities have been blunted by the Great War, and is also in large measure a result of that materialism which is engulfing our entire civilization.

GEORGE HORTON

Chapter 1

TURKISH MASSACRES, 1822–1909

MOHAMMEDANISM has been propagated by the sword and by violence ever since it first appeared as the great enemy of Christianity, as I shall show in a later chapter of this book.

It has been left to the Turk, however, in more recent years, to carry on the ferocious traditions of his creed, and to distinguish himself by excesses which have never been equaled by any of the tribes enrolled under the banner of the Prophet, either in ancient or in modern times.

The following is a partial list of Turkish massacres from 1822 up till 1904:

1822	Chios, Greeks	50,000
1823	Missolongi, Greeks	8,750
1826	Constantinople, Jannisaries	25,000
1850	Mosul, Assyrians	10,000
1860	Lebanon, Maronites	12,000
1876	Bulgaria, Bulgarians	14,700
1877	Bayazid, Armenians	1,400
1879	Alashguerd, Armenians	1,250
1881	Alexandria, Christians	2,000
1892	Mosul, Yezidies	3,500
1894	Sassun, Armenians	12,000
1895-96	Armenia, Armenians	150,000
1896	Constantinople, Armenians	9,570
1896	Van, Armenians	8,000
1903–04	Macedonia, Macedonians	14,667
1904	Sassun, Armenians	5,640
	Total	**328,477**

To this must be added the massacre in the province of Adana in 1909, of thirty thousand Armenians.

So imminent and ever-present was the peril, and so fresh the memory of these dire events in the minds of the non-Mussulman subjects of the sultan, that illiterate Christian mothers had fallen into the habit of dating events as so many years before or after "such and such a massacre."

Chapter 2

GLADSTONE AND THE BULGARIAN ATROCITIES

IN the list of massacres antedating the colossal crimes which have come under my own personal observation, is cited the killing of 14,700 Bulgarians in 1876. This butchery of a comparatively few—from a Turkish viewpoint—Bulgarians, some fifty years ago, provoked a splendid cry of indignation from Gladstone. As this narrative develops and reaches the dark days of 1915 to 1922, during which period whole nations were wiped out by the ax, the club and the knife, and the Turk at last found the opportunity to give full vent to his evil passions, it will appear that no similarly effective protest has issued from the lips of any European or American statesman.

The curious feature is that, owing to the propaganda carried on by the hunters of certain concessions, an anti-Christian and pro-Turk school has sprung up in the United States.

In *A Short History of the Near East*, Professor William Stearns Davis, of the University of Minnesota, referring to the Bulgarian atrocities 1876, says:

"What followed seems a massacre on a small scale compared with the slaughter of Armenians in 1915–16, but it was enough to paralyze the power of Disraeli to protect the Turks. In all, about twelve thousand Christians seem to have been massacred. At the thriving town of Batal five thousand out of seven thousand inhabitants seem to have perished. Of course neither age or sex was spared and lust and perfidy were added to other acts of devilishness. It is a pitiful commentary on a phase of British politics that Disraeli and his fellow Tories tried their best to minimize the reports of these atrocities. They were not given to the world by official consular reports, but by private English journalists."

The above is interesting, as it illustrates a quite common method of government procedure in such cases. The Tory does not seem to be a unique product of British politics.

While I was in Europe recently, I talked with a gentleman who was in the diplomatic service of one of the Great Powers and was with me in Smyrna at the time that city was burned by the Turkish army. This gentleman was in complete accord with me in all details as to that affair, and asserted that his Foreign Office had warned him to keep silent as to the real facts at Smyrna, but that he had written a full memorandum on the subject, which he hopes to publish.

It is significant that the Turks in 1876 were championed by Jews, while to-day such Jews as Henry Morgenthau, Max Nordau and Rabbi Wise are prominent among that group of men who are raising their voices in behalf of oppressed Christians. It is due to their influence, and to the voices of such senators as King of Utah and Swanson of Virginia, that confirmation of the Lausanne Treaty has been deferred until the blood on the bayonets and axes of the Turks should get a little drier.

Speaking of Disraeli, Gladstone wrote to the Duke of Argyle: "He is not such a Turk as I thought. What he hates is Christian liberty and reconstruction."

The Bulgarian massacres were made known by an American consular official, and denounced by Gladstone in a famous pamphlet. They led to the declaration of war by Russia, the treaty of San Stefano and the beginning of the freedom of Bulgaria.

In a speech at Blackheath in 1876, Gladstone said:

"You shall retain your titular sovereignty, your empire shall not be invaded, but never again, as the years roll in their course, so far as it is in our power to determine, never again shall the hand of violence be raised by you, never again shall the flood gates of lust be opened to you."

In his famous pamphlet, *Bulgarian Horrors and the Question of the East,* we have the following, a thousand times truer to-day than when it was written:

"Let the Turks now carry away their abuses, in the only possible manner, namely, by carrying off themselves. Their Zaptiehs and their Mudirs, their Bimbashis and Yuzbashis, their Kaimakams and their Pashas, one and all, bag and baggage, shall, I hope, clear out from the province that they have desolated and profaned. This thorough riddance, this most blessed deliverance, is the only reparation we can make to those heaps and heaps of dead, the violated purity alike of matron and of maiden and of child; to the civilization which has been affronted and shamed; to the laws of God, or, if you like, of Allah; to the moral sense of mankind at large.

There is not a criminal in an European jail, there is not a criminal in the South Sea Islands, whose indignation would not rise and overboil at the recital of that which has been done, which has too late been examined, but which remains unavenged, which has left behind all the foul and all the fierce passions which produced it and which may again spring up in another murderous harvest from the soil soaked and reeking with blood and in the air tainted with every imaginable deed of crime and shame. That such things should be done once is a damning disgrace to the portion of our race which did them; that the door should be left open to the ever so barely possible repetition would spread that shame over the world.

"We may ransack the annals of the world, but I know not what research can furnish us with so portentous an example of the fiendish misuse of the powers established by God for the punishment of evil doers and the encouragement of them that do well. No government ever has so sinned, none has proved itself so incorrigible in sin, or which is the same, so impotent in reformation."

The time will never come when the words of Gladstone, one of the wisest of English statesmen, will be considered unworthy of serious attention. The following characterization of the Turk by him has been more aptly verified by the events that have happened since his death than by those that occurred before:

"Let me endeavor, very briefly to sketch, in the rudest outline what the Turkish race was and what it is. It is not a question of Mohammedanism simply, but of Mohammedanism compounded with the peculiar character of a race. They are not the mild Mohammedans of India, nor the chivalrous Saladins of Syria, nor the cultured Moors of Spain. They were, upon the whole, from the black day when they first entered Europe, the one great anti-human specimen of humanity. Wherever they went a broad line of blood marked the track behind them, and, as far as their dominion reached, civilization disappeared from view. They represented everywhere government by force as opposed to government by law.—Yet a government by force can not be maintained without the aid of an intellectual element.— Hence there grew up, what has been rare in the history of the world, a kind of tolerance in the midst of cruelty, tyranny and rapine. Much of Christian life was contemptuously left alone and a race of Greeks was attracted to Constantinople which has

Rahmi Bey
Governor-General of Smyrna.

all along made up, in some degree, the deficiencies of Turkish Islam in the element of mind."

To these words of Gladstone may appropriately be added the characterization of the Turk by the famous Cardinal Newman:

"The barbarian power, which has been for centuries seated in the very heart of the Old World, which has in its brute clutch the most famous countries of classical and religious antiquity and many of the most fruitful and beautiful regions of the earth; and, which, having no history itself, is heir to the historical names of Constantinople and Nicaea, Nicomedia and Cæsarea, Jerusalem and Damascus, Nineva and Babylon, Mecca and Bagdad, Antioch and Alexandria, ignorantly holding in its possession one half of the history of the whole world."

In another passage Newman describes the Turk as the "great anti-Christ among the races of men."

Chapter 3

FIRST STEP IN YOUNG TURKS' PROGRAM
(1908–1911)

TO comprehend this narrative thoroughly, one must remember that the East is unchangeable. The Turks of to-day are precisely the same as those who followed Mohammed the Conqueror through the gates of Constantinople on May 29, 1453, and they have amply demonstrated that they do not differ from those whom Gladstone denounced for the Bulgarian atrocities of 1876. Those who are building hopes on any other conception will be deceived; they will be painfully deceived if they make treaties or invest large sums of money on Western ideas of the Oriental character.

I am neither "pro-Greek," "pro-Turk," nor anything except pro-American and pro-Christ. Having passed the most of my life in regions where race feeling runs high, it has been my one aim to help the oppressed, irrespective of race, as will be shown by documents submitted later, and I have won the expressed gratitude of numerous Turks for the aid and relief I have afforded them on various occasions.

I am aware of the many noble qualities of the Turkish peasant, but I do not agree with many precepts of his religion, and I do not admire him when he is cutting throats or violating Christian women. The massacres already enumerated are a sufficient blot upon the Turkish name. They were made possible by the teachings of the Koran, the example of Mohammed, lust and the desire for plunder. They sink into insignificance when compared with the vast slaughter of more recent years, conducted under the auspices of Abdul Hamid, Talaat and Company, and Mustapha Khemal.

It should be borne in mind, however, that it was not until after the declaration of the constitution that the idea "Turkey for the Turks" took definite shape and developed into the scheme of accomplishing its purpose by the final extinction of all the Christian populations of that blood-soaked land—a plan consistent with, and a continuation of, the general history of Mohammedan expansion in the ancient home lands of Christianity.

At the time of the declaration of the constitution in 1908, I was in Athens. My first intimation of the event was a procession of Greeks carrying Hellenic and Ottoman flags, marching through the streets on their way to the Turkish legation, where they made a friendly and enthusiastic demonstration.

The idea in Greece and the Balkans generally was that the constitution meant equal rights for all in Turkey, irrespective of religion—the dawn of a new era. Had this conception proved true, Turkey would to-day be one of the great, progressive, prosperous countries of the world. The weakness of the conception was that in an equal and friendly rivalry, the Christians would speedily have outstripped the Ottomans, who would soon have found themselves in a subordinate position commercially, industrially and economically. It was this knowledge which caused the Turks to resolve upon the extermination of the Christians. It was a reversal of the process of nature; the drones were about to kill off the working bees.

During these days a member of the Turkish Cabinet made a speech at Saloniki, advocating the closing of all the foreign missionary schools, as well as native Christian, arguing: "If we close the Christian institutions, Turkish institutions will of necessarily spring up to take their place. A country must have schools."

Immediately after the fall of Abdul Hamid, I was transferred to Saloniki. There was great rejoicing over the fall of the "Bloody Tyrant," and the certainty prevailed that the subjects of Turkey had at last united to form a kingdom where all should have full liberty to worship God and pursue their peaceful occupations in security. The fall of Abdul Hamid had been made possible by the cooperation and aid of the Christians.

But the latter—Greeks, Bulgars, Serbs—were soon cruelly disillusioned. A general persecution was started, the details of which were reported to their various governments by all the consuls of the city. This persecution first displayed itself in the form of sporadic murders of alarming frequency all over Macedonia, the victims being, in the beginning, notables of the various Christian communities. A favorite place for shooting these people was at their doorsteps at the moment of their return home. It became evident that the Turkish Government, in order to gain control of the territory, was bent upon the extermination of the non-Mussulman leaders. Many of those murdered had been prominent in the anti-Abdul movement.

From the extermination of notables, the program extended to people of less importance, who began to disappear. Bevies of despairing peasant women who had come to visit the *vali* (Turkish governor) and demand news of their husbands, sons or brothers, appeared on the streets of Saloniki. The answers were usually sardonic; "He has probably run away and left you," or "He has probably gone to America," were favorite replies. The truth, however, could not long be hidden, as shepherds and others were soon reporting corpses found in ravines and gullies in the mountains and woods. The reign of terror, the Turks' immemorial method of rule, was on in earnest, and the next step taken to generalize it was the so-called "disarming". This meant, as always, the disarming of the Christian element, and the furnishing of weapons to the Turks.

An order was issued that all persons must give up their guns and other weapons, and squads of soldiers were sent out through villages to put this edict into effect. That the object was not so much to collect hidden arms as to terrorize the inhabitants was soon made evident from the tortures inflicted during the search. Bastinadoing was a favorite measure. The feet of the peasants, accustomed to going barefoot, were very tough; they were therefore tied down and their toes beaten to a pulp with clubs.

Another form of torment frequently resorted to by the "Government of Union and Progress," was tying a rope around the victim's waist and slipping a musket between the body and the cord and twisting until internal injury resulted. Priests were frequent victims of this campaign of terror and hate, the idea being to render them ridiculous as well as to inflict hideous suffering. The poor creatures were made to stand upon one foot while a soldier menaced them with a bayonet. If the priest, finally exhausted, dropped the upraised foot to the ground, he was stabbed with the bayonet.

The prisons were bursting with unfortunate people existing in starvation and filth. An American tobacco merchant related to me that a prominent Greek merchant disappeared from the streets and for several days screams were heard issuing from the second story of a certain building. This Greek was not killed, but was finally released. He showed the American round pits all over his body. He had been tied naked to a table and hot oil dropped on him. When he had asked, in his agony, "What have I done!" his persecutors replied, "We

are doing this to show you that Turkey has been freed for the Turks."
He was doubtless let go to spread the glad news.

A well-known British correspondent, a pro-Bulgar, stated that he
had sent reports of these persecutions to the British press, but could
not get them published. He had the obsession that the reason was
because the whole British press was owned by Jews, but it is not easy
to follow him in this deduction. The true reason is to be found in
some government policy of the moment.

It was this indiscriminate persecution of Greeks, Bulgars and
Serbs which drove them into the same camp and enabled them to
chase the Turk out of Macedonia, even though they did fall at one
another's throats as soon as they got rid of the common enemy. Any
one inclined to doubt the veracity of the above description must
understand, if he knows anything of Balkan matters, that it needed a
pretty serious state of affairs to cause Greek and Bulgar to fight on the
same side.

The persecution to which all the races in the Empire were
subjected, with the exception of the Turks, is well-depicted in the
following article in the *Nea Aletheia*, a conservative journal published
in the Greek language, in Saloniki, which used all its influence in
favor of harmony and moderation. The following is from the issue of
July 10, 1910, or about two years after the declaration of the famous
"Constitution":

"Before two years are finished a secret committee is unearthed in
Constantinople, with branches all over in important commercial
towns, whose intentions are declared to be subversive of the present
state of affairs. In this committee are found many prominent men
and members of Congress. All discontent seen in the kingdom has its
beginning in this perverted policy. Our rulers, according to their
newly adopted system of centralization upon the basis of the
domination of the ruling race have given gall and wormwood to all
the other races. They have displeased the Arabs by wishing them to
abandon their language. They have alienated the Albanians by
attempting to apply force, though conciliatory measures would have
been better. They have dissatisfied the Armenians by neglecting their
lawful petitions. They have offended the Bulgarians by forcing them
to live with foreigners brought purposely from other places. They
have dissatisfied the Serbians by using against them measures the
harshness of which is contrary to human laws.

"But for us Greeks words are useless. We have every day before us such a vivid picture of persecution and extermination that however much we might say, would not be sufficient to express the magnitude of the misfortunes, which since two years have come upon our heads. It is acknowledged that the Greek race ranks second as a pillar of the Constitution and that it is the most valuable of those contributing to the prosperity of the Ottoman fatherland.

"We have the right to ask, what have we, Ottoman Greeks, done that we should be so persecuted? The law-abiding character of the Ottoman Greeks is indisputable. To us were given promises that our rights would remain untouched. Despite this, laws are voted through which churches, schools, and cemeteries belonging to us are taken and given to others. Clergymen and teachers are imprisoned, citizens are beaten, from everywhere lamentation and weeping are heard.

"With what joy we Ottoman Greeks hailed the rise of the 10th of July! With what eagerness we took part in the expedition of April, 1909! With what hopes we look forward even to-day to the future of this country! It is ours, and no power is able to separate us from it.

"The Greeks are a power in Turkey; a moral and material power. This power is impossible for our compatriot Turks to ignore. When will that day come when full agreement will exist between the two races! Then only hand in hand will both march forward, and Turkey will reach the height which is her due."

The following is from my Saloniki diary, dated December 11, 1910:

"Wholesale arrests, in some of the towns all the prominent citizens being thrown into jail together.

"Series of assassinations of chiefs of communities, in broad day, in the streets. Fifty prominent Bulgarians thus shot down, and many Greeks.

"The following figures were obtained from a report of the Turkish Parliament and locally confirmed:

"In the Sandjack of Uskub, 1,104 persons bastinadoed; Villayet of Monastir, 285 persons bastinadoed; Saloniki, 464 persons bastinadoed; (of these 11 died and 62 were permanently injured.) Casas of Yenidje-Vardar, Gevgeli, Vodena, 911 persons were bastinadoed.

"All the prisons are crowded with Christians; many have fled into Bulgaria and thousands of men, women and children are hiding in the mountains."

This was the state of affairs two years after the declaration of the Constitution, and it was this common suffering which Greeks, Bulgars and Serbians endured, which drove them together and forced them to declare the First Balkan War, in October of 1912, in which the Turk was practically driven out of Europe until Christian statesmen of the Great Powers brought him back again. Turkish power has always been built upon Christian dissension and aid.

In the (at that time) pro-Turk *Progres de Salonique*, a journal published in the French language at Saloniki, appeared an article which expresses a state of feeling among Oriental peoples which has taken great distension since the date of the article (July 22, 1910). What was then a fire bids fair now to grow into a general conflagration, due to the building up, by Christian powers, of the sinister puissance of Mustapha Khemal:

"In the space of three years," says the article, "the Orient, twice and from its two extremities, has marvelously astonished the civilized world: first, by the great victory won by the Japanese over the strongest of Occidental peoples, and next by the wonderful revolution in Turkey! In fact, it is a marvel, which is being accomplished to-day! There is no comparison between the Orient of to-day and that of ten years ago. What is more curious is that this Oriental movement has taken the form of two separate currents, which, starting from the two extremities of the Orient, are going to meet and their points of junction will be, in all probability, India."

"At the head of these movement will be found the peoples belonging to the same race—the Mongolians. Each one possesses the unquestionable title to the moral and intellectual supremacy of the great countries over which their influence extends."

"The Japanese are incontestably at the head of the peoples professing Buddhism, the doctrine of Confucius, etc.; the Turks, defenders of Islam for centuries, are the incontestable leaders of the people professing Islamism. Therefore, the two movements, starting from the two extremities of Asia, from the Bosphoros and Tokio, go spreading, each one in an appropriate field prepared in advance by history itself to accept it, then, since they are essentially the same, they will unite at their point of junction, to form a common and formidable Asiatic current. With this in view, the Occident is feeling uneasy and agitated."

Immediately after the reestablishment of the Constitution, then, the first step of the dominant race was to solidify its supremacy by measures of suppression, oppression, and murder. The Turks also deliberately undertook to force all the non-Turkish races to become in language, laws, habits and almost all other particulars, "Ottomans."[*]

It is exactly this policy, in operation, which is referred to in the clipping from the *Nea Aletheia,* quoted above. A more foolish project was never conceived by the mind of man—that of forcing whole nations to change their languages and habits overnight. The impossibility of this scheme becomes all the more evident when the reader reflects that an inferior civilization was attempting to impose itself upon a superior one. The Turk never had any intention of giving equal liberty to all the peoples who were so unfortunate as to be in his power. Failing to "Turkify" them, as it has been called, his only next alternative was to massacre and drive them out, a policy not long in developing.

---

[*] Professor Davis' *Short History of the Near East.*

Chapter 4

THE LAST GREAT SELAMLIK
(1911)

A PICTURESQUE incident in the process of "Turkifying" took place in Macedonia in May and June of 1911. Mehmet V arrived in Saloniki on May thirty-first of that year on a battle-ship escorted by the greater part of the Turkish fleet. It had been known for some days that he was coming, as his advance guard, in the shape of tall flabby eunuchs, cooks, etc., began to appear and lounge about in front of the principal hotels. The town was liberally beflagged, and the different communities made demonstrations in his honor, the Bulgarians showing especial enthusiasm. He visited Uskub and Monastir and, from the former place, proceeded to the Plain of Kossovo, where the decisive battle was fought, which brought the Turks and the Turkish blight into Europe. There on June 15, 1389, the Sultan Amurath defeated the heroic Lazarus, King of the Serbians. This Turkish victory, whose evil consequences have lasted down into our own times, was made possible by treachery of Christian allies, the real cause of all Turkish triumphs.

Amurath himself was slain, and it was in the plain where are found his simple monument and a mosque in commemoration of his name, that Mehmet V, the witless dotard and befuddled puppet of the Young Turk Committee, called together all the various picturesque tribes of Turkey in Europe for a grand *selamlik,* or service of prayer.

Besides civilians, some of whom are said to have walked for days to be present, there were thousands of troops, and many famous regiments, carrying ancient battletorn flags. A huge tent had been erected for the sultan, and the vast throng seated itself upon the ground. As the priests recited the service and the thousands of worshippers bent their foreheads to the earth and sat up again, the sea of red fezzes rose and fell rhythmically like a wide field of poppies swayed by the wind.

There have been in the world's history few more picturesque and impressive sights than this last *selamlik* on the ill-omened "Plain of Blackbirds."

I was presented to Mehmet (or Mohámmed V) at Saloniki, and a more flabby, pitiful, witless countenance it would be difficult to imagine. The bleary eyes were puffy underneath, the lower lip dropped in slobbery fashion. His Imperial Majesty was accompanied by several shrewd-faced prompters, of the Europeanized type, and he never uttered a word without turning to one of them with a helpless and infantile expression for directions as to what to say or do. When the interview was finished, Mehmet turned his back and started to walk away. He had gone but a few steps when one of the prompters whispered to him, whereupon he faced about ponderously and slowly twisted his features into a ghastly and mechanical grin. It was as clear as any pantomime could be made that he had been instructed to smile when taking leave, and had forgotten a part of his lesson.

Mehmet V had been kept in confinement all his life, practically, by his brother, the great and cruel Abdul, by whom it was said that he had been encouraged to absorb daily incredible quantities of *raki*. He was a kindly harmless soul, who had been selected by Enver and the rest because he had become practically an imbecile.

The great *selamlik* made a strong appeal to the Turks, deeply stirring their religious feelings, but it is needless to say that it did not accomplish much "Turkeifying" the Christian element. And all this time the crafty Abdul, the fatuous "Sick Man" of Europe, one of the greatest diplomats and murderers in the history of the world, was confined with a small array of wives in the Villa Allatini at Saloniki.

Chapter 5

PERSECUTION OF CHRISTIANS IN SMYRNA DISTRICT

(1911–1914)

IN 1911, I was transferred to Smyrna, where I remained till May of 1917, when the Turks ruptured relations with the United States. During the period from 1914 to 1917, I was in charge of the Entente interests in Asia Minor and was in close contact with Rahmi Bey, the famous and shrewd war governor-general.

The Greek subjects in Asia Minor were not disturbed for the reason, as explained by Rahmi Bey, that King Constantine was in reality an ally of Turkey and that he was preventing Greece from going into the war. The Rayas, or Greek Ottoman subjects, of the Port were, on the other hand, abominably treated. These people were the expert artisans, principal merchants and professional men of the cities, and the skilled and progressive farmers of the country. It was they who introduced the cultivation of the famous Sultanina raisins, improved the curing and culture of tobacco, and built modern houses and pretty towns. They were rapidly developing a civilization that would ultimately have approached the classic days of Ionia. A general boycott was declared against them, for one thing, and posters calling on the Mussulmans to exterminate them were posted in the schools and mosques. The Turkish newspapers also published violent articles exciting their readers to persecution and massacre. A meeting of the consular corps was held and the decision was taken to visit the *vali* and call the attention of His Excellency to the danger that these articles and this agitation might disturb the tranquility of a peaceful province.

The consuls visited the *vali*, with the exception of the German representative, who alleged that he could not join in such a move without the express authorization of his government. This action of the German official on the spot is another confirmation of the assertion that Germany was to a large extent co-guilty with her Turkish allies in the matter of the deportations and massacres of Christians. In fact, there is little doubt that Germany inspired the expulsion of the Ottoman Greeks of Asia Minor at that time, as one of the preliminary moves in the war, which she was preparing.

The ferocious expulsion and terrorizing by murder and violence of the Rayas along the Asia Minor littoral, which has not attracted the attention it merits, has all the earmarks of a war measure, prompted by alleged "military necessity," and there is no doubt that Turks and Germans were allies during the war and were in complete cooperation. A study of this question may be found in Publication No. 3, of the American Hellenic Society, 1918, in which the statement is made that one million, five hundred thousand Greeks were driven from their homes in Thrace and Asia Minor, and that half these populations had perished from deportations, outrages and famine.

The violent and inflammatory articles in the Turkish newspapers, above referred to, appeared unexpectedly and without any cause. They were so evidently "inspired" by the authorities, that it seems a wonder that even ignorant Turks did not understand this. Cheap lithographs were also got up, executed in the clumsiest and most primitive manner—evidently local productions. They represented Greeks cutting up Turkish babies or ripping open pregnant Moslem women, and various purely imaginary scenes, founded on no actual events or even accusations elsewhere made. These were hung in the mosques and schools. This campaign bore immediate fruit and set the Turk to killing, a not very difficult thing to do.

A series of sporadic murders began at Smyrna as at Saloniki, the list in each morning's paper numbering from twelve to twenty. Peasants going into their vineyards to work were shot down from behind trees and rocks by the Turks. One peculiarly atrocious case comes to mind: Two young men, who had recently finished their studies in a high-grade school, went out to a vineyard to pass the night in the *coula* (house in the country). During the night they were called to the door and chopped down with axes. Finally the Rayas, to the number of several hundred thousand, were all driven off from their farms or out of their villages. Some were deported into the interior, but many managed to escape by means of *caiques* to the neighboring islands, whence they spread over Greece. A few thousand Turks destroyed the region, which the Greeks were developing and rendering fertile, from Pergamus clear down the coast to Lidja. I went over the whole region and took photographs of the

The Long Line that Leads to Death.
Deportation of Christians from their homes to the arid wastes to die.

ruined farmhouses and villages. Goats had been turned into flourishing, carefully tended vine-yards and acres of roots had been dug up for fuel.

Most of the Christian houses in Asia Minor are built of a wooden framework, which serves as an earthquake proof skeleton for the walls of stone and mortar. The Turks pulled the houses down by laying a timber across the inside of the window—or door-frame—to which a team of buffaloes or oxen was hitched. A Turk would reside in one of the houses with his wife, or with his goats and cattle, and thus tear down a circle of houses about him. When the radius became too great for convenience, he moved into the center of another cluster of houses. The object of destroying the houses was to get the wooden timbers for firewood.

Both at this time and during the progress of the Great War, the Rayas were drafted into the army where they were treated as slaves. They were not given guns, but were employed to dig trenches and do similar work, and as they were furnished neither food, clothing nor shelter, large numbers of them perished of hunger and exposure.

The beginning of the work on the "Great Turkish Library" at Smyrna was peculiarly interesting as a revelation of the mentality of the race. Christians were used for the labor, the taskmasters, of course, being Turks armed with whips. When I called the attention of Rahmi Bey, the governor-general, one day to the fact that there were not sufficient books existing in his native tongue to justify the construction of so great an edifice, he replied: "The first thing is to have a building. If we have a building the books will necessarily appear to fill it, and even if they don't, we are going to translate all the German books into Turkish."

The structure was never finished, and consequently the books have not been written.

Chapter 6

THE MASSACRE OF PHOCEA
(1914)

THE complete and documentary account of the ferocious persecutions of the Christian population of the Smyrna region, which occurred in 1914, is not difficult to obtain; but it will suffice, by way of illustration, to give only some extracts from a report by the French eye-witness, Manciet, concerning the massacre and pillage of Phocea, a town of eight thousand Greek inhabitants and about four hundred Turks, situated on the sea a short distance from Smyrna. The destruction of Phocea excited great interest in Marseilles, as colonists of the very ancient Greek town founded the French city. Phocea is the mother of Marseilles. Monsieur Manciet was present at the massacre and pillage of Phocea, and, together with three other Frenchmen, Messieurs Sartiaux, Carlier and Dandria, saved hundreds of lives by courage and presence of mind.

The report begins with the appearance on the hills behind the town of armed bands and the firing of shots, causing a panic. Those four gentlemen were living together, but when the panic commenced they separated and each installed himself in a house. They demanded of the Kaimakam gendarmes for their protection, and each obtained one. They kept the doors open and gave refuge to all who came. They improvised four French flags out of cloth and flew one from each house. But, to continue the recital in Monsieur Manciet's own words, translated from the French:

"During the night the organized bands continued the pillage of the town. At the break of dawn there was continual *très nourrie* firing before the houses. Going out immediately, we four, we saw the most atrocious spectacle of which it is possible to dream. This horde, which had entered the town, was armed with Gras rifles and cavalry muskets. A house was in flames. From all directions the Christians were rushing to the quays seeking boats to get away in, but since the night there were none left. Cries of terror mingled with the sound of firing. The panic was so great that a woman with her child was drowned in sixty centimeters of water.

"Mr. Carlier saw an atrocious spectacle. A Christian stood at his door, which the bandits wished to enter, as his wife and daughter were in the

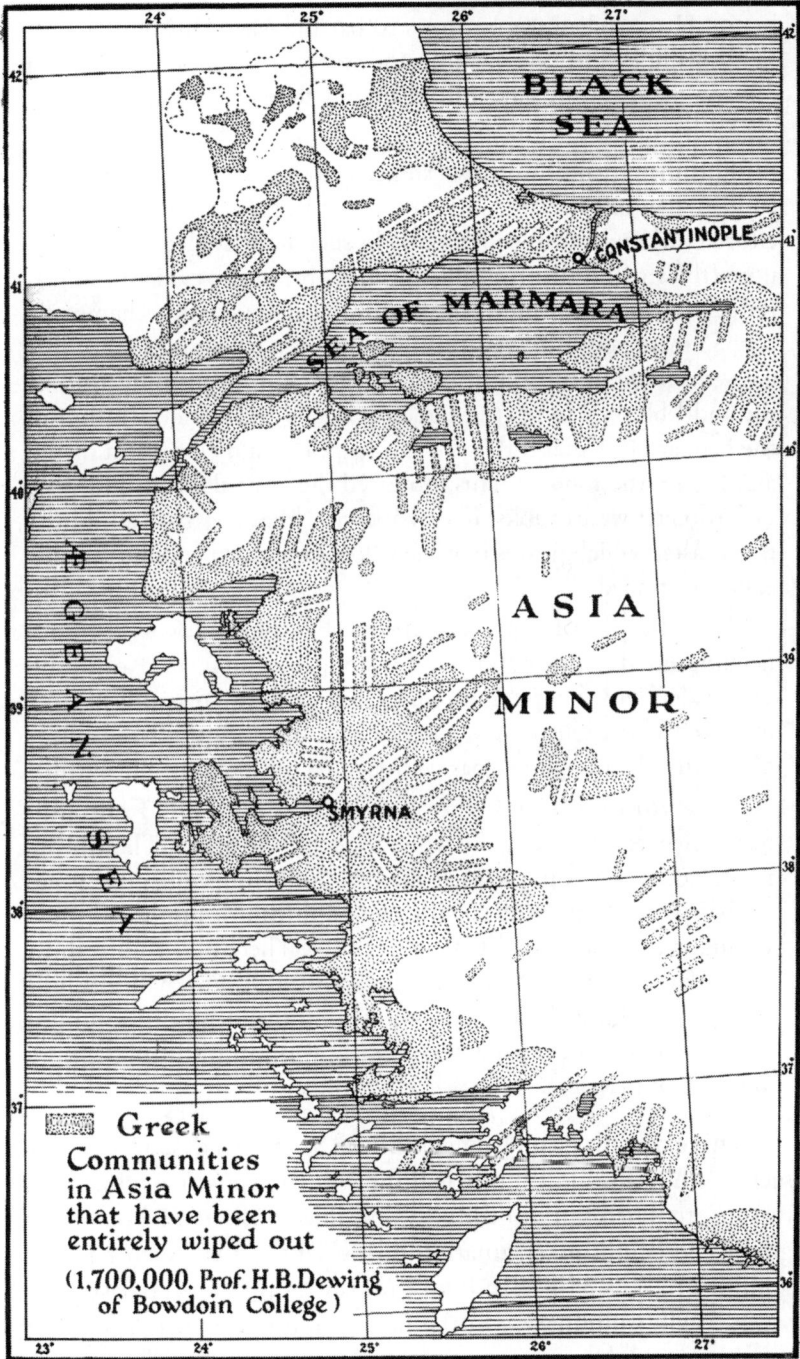

BLACK
SEA

CONSTANTINOPLE

SEA OF MARMARA

AEGEAN SEA

ASIA

MINOR

SMYRNA

Greek
Communities
in Asia Minor
that have been
entirely wiped out
(1,700,000. Prof. H.B.Dewing
of Bowdoin College)

house. He stretched out his arms to bar the way. This motion cost him his life for they shot him in the stomach. As he was staggering toward the sea, they gave him a second shot in the back, and the corpse lay there for two days.

"Fortunately there were two steamers in port, and we managed to embark the unfortunate Christians in small groups. Despite all our efforts, these wretched people were in such haste to depart that they upset the small boats. An odious detail proved the cynicism of this horde, which, under pretext of disarming those leaving, shamefully robbed these poor, terrified people of their last belongings. They tore away from old women packages and bedding by force. Anger seized me and I blushed to see these abominations and I told an officer of the gendarmerie that if this did not stop, I would take a gun myself and fire on the robbers. This produced the desired effect, and these unfortunates were enabled to embark with what they had saved from the disaster, which proves that the whole movement could have been easily controlled.

"But the plundering was stopped only in our immediate neighborhood. Farther away we saw doors broken in and horses and asses laden with booty. This continued all day. Toward evening I mounted a little hill and saw a hundred camels laden with the pillage of the city. That night we passed in agony, but nothing happened.

"The following day the methodical pillage of the city recommenced. And now the wounded began to arrive. There being no doctor, I took upon myself the first aid before embarking them for Mitylene. I affirm that with two or three exceptions, all these wounded were more than sixty years of age. There were among them aged women, more than ninety years of age, who had received gunshots, and it is difficult to imagine that they had been wounded while defending their possessions. It was simply and purely a question of massacre."

   This extract is given from Monsieur Manciet's description of the sack of Phocea in 1914, of which he was an eye-witness, for several reasons. It is necessary to the complete and substantiated picture the gradual ferocious extermination of the Christians which had been going on in Asia Minor and the Turkish Empire for the past several years, finally culminating in the horror of Smyrna; it is a peculiarly graphic recital, bringing out the unchanging nature of the Turk and his character as a creature of savage passions, living still in the times

The Christians of this region, principally Greeks, numbered 250,000 (Dr. Karl Dietrich in "Griechentum Klein Asien") They have been exterminated or driven out.

of Tamerlane or Attila, the Hun;—for the Turk is an anachronism; still looting, killing and raping and carrying off his spoil on camels; it is peculiarly significant, also, as it tells a story strongly resembling some of the exploits of Mohammed himself; it also gives a clear idea of what happened over the entire coast of Asia Minor and far back into the interior in 1914, temporarily destroying a flourishing and rapidly growing civilization, which was later restored by the advent of the Greek army, only to go out in complete darkness under the bloody and lustful hands of the followers of Mustapha Khemal; it rings again the constant note, so necessary to be understood by the European or American, that this was an "organized movement," as Monsieur Manciet says:

"We found an old woman lying in the street, who had been nearly paralyzed by blows. She had two great wounds on the head made by the butts of muskets; her hands were cut, her face swollen.

"A young girl, who had given all the money she possessed, had been thanked by knife stabs, one in the arm and the other in the region of the kidneys. A weak old man had received such a blow with a gun that the fingers of his left hand had been carried away.

"From all directions during the day that followed families arrived that had been hidden in the mountains. All had been attacked. Among them was a woman who had seen killed, before her eyes, her husband, her brother and her three children.

"We learned at this moment an atrocious detail. An old paralytic, who had been lying helpless on his bed at the moment the pillagers entered, had been murdered.

"Smyrna sent us soldiers to establish order. As these soldiers circulated in the streets, we had a spectacle of the kind of order which they established; they continued, personally, the sacking of the town.

"We made a tour of inspection through the city. The pillage was complete; doors were broken down and that which the robbers had not been able to carry away they had destroyed. Phocea, which had been a place of great activity, was now a dead city.

"A woman was brought to us dying; she had been violated by seventeen Turks. They had also carried off into the mountains a girl of sixteen, having murdered her father and mother before her eyes. We had seen, therefore, as in the most barbarous times, the five characteristics of the sacking of a city; theft, pillage, fire, murder and rape.

"All ·the evidence points to this having been an organized attack with the purpose of driving from the shores the Rayas, or Christian Ottomans.

"It is inconceivable that all these persons should have had in their possession so many army weapons if they had not been given them. As for the Christians of old Phocea, there was not for one instant an effort at defense. It was, therefore, a carnage.

"We read in the journals that order had been established, and that, in the regions of which we speak, the Christians have nothing further to fear, neither for themselves, nor for their possessions. This is not a vain statement. Order reigns, for nobody is left. The possessions have nothing further to fear, for they are all in good hands—those of the robbers."

Chapter 7

NEW LIGHT ON THE
ARMENIAN MASSACRES
(1914–1915)

IN 1915, the time of the vast extermination of Armenians, Consul Jesse B. Jackson was stationed at Aleppo, and greatly distinguished himself by the aid, which he gave those unfortunate people. As Consul Jackson was in these horrible scenes, it would be interesting to read his reports, if they were obtainable, but unfortunately they are not. Quotation can fortunately be made from the account, here published for the first time, of a native-born American citizen who was at Aleppo and was an eye-witness of the things which he describes:

"The forerunner of events in which the unfortunate Armenians were to be massacred and forced to undergo the most severe hardships occurred at Zeitun, a town situated about five days' journey north of Aleppo, in February, 1915, when, with great reluctance, the Armenians were made to submit to disarmament by the Turks. Following the Zeitun incident, similar action was taken in Aintab, Alexandretta, Marash, Urfa, etc.

"Shortly after the disarmament of the Armenians in the above-mentioned places, the deportations began, which were so destructive to the Armenian race and were carried out on orders from the Turkish officials in Constantinople.

"Throughout the terrible days of the deportation, Consul Jackson was repeatedly called upon to render assistance and to use every effort to prevent the deportation of any one in Aleppo. This, during the time when he represented fifteen different countries and was protecting their various interests. (This was during the war, of course, before Turkey severed relations with the United States.) It can be readily seen that his position was a very delicate one, and every move on his part had to be made with the utmost care in order not to call down upon him and especially his assistants, the displeasure of the Turkish authorities.

"While Consul Jackson was endeavoring to the best of his ability to stop a massacre in Aleppo, news began to leak in of the terrible atrocities that were occurring in connection with the deportations from Sivas,

Harput, Trebizonde, Bitlis, Diarbekir, Mardin, Cæsarea, Konia, Adana, Mersina and other cities and towns in the district.

"Gradually small numbers sent away from the above mentioned towns began to arrive in Aleppo, relating the harrowing details of the deportations, or the actual killing of relatives and friends, or the unbelievable brutalities of the gendarmes toward young girls, and more attractive women, or the carrying off by Turks and Kurds of beautiful girls and countless other atrocious crimes committed against them.

"One of the most terrible sights ever witnessed in Aleppo was the arrival, early in August, 1915, of some five thousand terribly emaciated, dirty, ragged and sick women and children, three thousand on one day and two thousand the following day. These people were the only survivors of the thrifty and prosperous Armenians of the province of Sivas, carefully estimated to have been originally over three hundred thousand souls. And what became of the balance? From the most intelligent of those that reached Aleppo, it was learned that in early spring of 1915 the men and boys over fourteen years old had been called to the police stations in that province on different mornings stretching over a period of several weeks and had been sent off in groups of from one thousand to two thousand each, tied together with ropes and that nothing had ever been heard of them thereafter. Their fate has been recorded in the annals of God, so is needless to dwell thereon here. These survivors related the most harrowing experiences that they endured en route, parting from their homes as they did before Easter, traveling perhaps a thousand miles and reaching Aleppo in August, about four months afterward, afoot, without sufficient food, and even denied drink by the brutal gendarmes when they came to the wells by the way side. Hundreds of the prettiest women and girls had been stolen by the Turkish tribes who came among them every day."

Of the fate of the men and boys over fourteen, who were carried away and never heard of again, many corroborating accounts were received at Smyrna. It is certain that they were killed, the Turks chopping many of them to death with axes, to save ammunition.

As we are still dealing with the systematic extermination of Christians previous to the burning of Smyrna by the Turks, a few pages will be devoted to the destruction of the Armenian nation, the most horrible crime in the history of the human race in its details of lust and savagery and suffering, as well as in extent, and which definitely outlaws its perpetrators from the society of human beings and from the fellowship of civilized nations, until such time as full repentance is convincingly shown and an honest effort made, in so far as possible, to make reparation.

There have probably been destructive movements that have cost more lives than that of the extermination of the Christians by the Turks. Tamerlane, for instance, swept over vast stretches of country, killing and burning for the mere love of destruction. He spared neither Mussulman nor Christian. But there were features of fiendish cruelty and long-drawn-out suffering in the Ottoman persecution of the Christians that did not characterize the methods of Tamerlane.

Reference will be made to the most notable official collections of evidence on the subject, and two important documents, reports of American eye-witnesses, will be given. These latter have never before been published. One of the fullest and most reliable sources of information on the Armenian massacres is the official publication of the British Parliament, 1915 entitled *The Treatment of the Armenians,* containing documents presented to Viscount Grey of Falloden, Secretary of State for Foreign Affairs, by Viscount Bryce. A copy can be found in the Library of Congress, at Washington. These documents really constitute a large volume, giving evidence from all sources as to the Armenian butcheries amid extermination by slow torture. Much of the testimony here given is so revolting, and so outrages all human feelings and sensibilities, that one refrains from quoting it.

Lord Grey, then British Secretary of State, on receiving these documents, wrote to Viscount Bryce:

> "My Dear Bryce: It is a terrible mass of evidence, but I feel it ought to be published and widely studied by all who have the broad interests of humanity at heart. It will be valuable, not only for the immediate information of public opinion as to the conduct of the Turkish Government toward this defenseless people, but also as a mine of information for historians in the future.
>
> (Signed) GREY OF FALLODEN"

Various opinions of distinguished people are given as to the credibility of this evidence. Among others, Gilbert Murray, the famous scholar and poet, says: "The evidence of these letters and reports will bear any scrutiny and overpower any skepticism."

An expert on the matter of evidence, Moorfield Storey, formerly President of the American Bar Association, writes cautiously but conclusively:

"In my opinion, the evidence which you print is as reliable as that upon which rests our belief in many of the universally accepted facts of history, and I think it establishes beyond any reasonable doubt the deliberate purpose of the Turkish authorities practically to exterminate the Armenians, and their responsibility for the hideous atrocities which have been perpetrated upon that unhappy people."

Other works to be consulted in this connection, filled with corroborating and overwhelming testimony are: *Beginning Again at Ararat,* by Doctor Mabel E. Elliott; *Shall This Nation Die,* by Reverend Joseph Naayem; and most convincing of all, the *Secret Report on the Massacres of Armenia,* by Doctor Johannes Lepsius, German missionary and President of the German Orient Mission. Doctor Lepsius' explanation of the necessity for the secrecy of his report, which was made to his "friends of the mission," is illuminating:

"Dear Friends of the Mission: The following report which I am sending to you absolutely confidentiality, has been printed as a manuscript. It can not, either as a whole or in part, be given to the public, nor utilized. The censor can not authorize, during the war, publications concerning events in Turkey. Our political and military interests oblige us with imperious demands. Turkey is our ally. In addition to having defended her own country, she has rendered service to us ourselves by her valiant defense of the Dardanelles. Our fraternity of arms with Turkey imposes, then, obligations, but it does not hinder us from fulfilling the duties of humanity. But, if we must be quiet in public, our conscience does not, however, cease to speak. The most ancient people of Christianity is in danger of being wiped out, in so far as it is in the power of the Turks; six sevenths of the Armenian people have been despoiled of their possessions, driven from their fire-sides, and, in so far as they have not accepted Islam, have been killed or deported into the desert. The same fate has happened to the Nestorians of Syria, and part of the Greek Christians have suffered."

Doctor Lepsius prepares his report in the manner of true German scholar. It is detailed, exhaustive and authoritative.

A prominent foreign official, not a German, has already been mentioned, who was constrained to keep silent as to Turkish atrocities. How strong the Turk is! He can do what he pleases, can break all the laws of God and man, and everybody, for some reason or other, must keep quiet about it. A redeeming feature of German complicity in the Armenian horrors was the acquittal by a German court of the Armenian who wreaked justice upon Talaat Bey. It is said that the testimony of German missionaries influenced the court to render that judgment.

The heart-rending and harrowing details of the wholesale murder of the Armenians can be drawn out indefinitely. Suffice it to say that, in addition to actual and repeated killings on a grand scale, the plan of doing to death by the slow torture of deportation is one of the most devilish that depraved and fiendish brains have ever conceived.

A fresh contribution to the subject confirmatory of all that has hitherto been written is the report of Walter M. Geddes, of the MacAndrews and Forbes Company, of New York, which was handed to me by Mr. Geddes a short time before his unfortunate death in Smyrna. Mr. Geddes being dead, no fear exists of prejudicing him with the Turks by using his name. It is perhaps the most remarkable account of a great historic massacre by slow torture that has ever been written, and derives its vividness of detail from the fact that the writer describes the things that he actually saw.

Chapter 8

STORY OF WALTER M. GEDDES

"I LEFT here on the sixteenth of September, 1915, for Aleppo. I first saw the Armenians at Afion Karahissar where there was a big encampment— probably of ten thousand people—who had come down from the Black Sea. They were encamped in tents made of material of all descriptions, and their condition was deplorable.

"The next place I saw them was at Konia, also a large encampment. There I saw the first brutality; I saw a woman and her baby separated from her husband; he was put on our train while she was forcibly held behind and kept from getting on the train.

"The next place where there was a large encampment was at Osmanieh, where there was said to be about fifty thousand; their condition was terrible. They were camped on both sides of the railway track, extending fully half a mile on each side. Here they had two wells from whence they could get water, one of which was very far from the encampment, the other at the railway station platform. At daybreak, the Armenians came in crowds, women and children and old men, to get to the well to get water. They fought among themselves for a place at the well, and the gendarmes, to keep them in order, whipped several people. I saw women and children repeatedly struck with whips and sticks in the hands of the gendarmes. Later I had occasion to pass through the camp on the way to the town of Osmanieh and had an opportunity to see the condition of the people. They were living in tents like those above described and their condition was miserable. The site of the encampment had been used several times by different caravans of Armenians and no attempt at sanitation had been made by either the Turks or the Armenians themselves, with the result that the ground was in a deplorable condition, and the stench in the early morning was beyond description. At Osmanieh, they were selling their possessions in order to obtain money to buy food. One old man begged me to buy his silver snuffbox for a piaster in order that he might be able to buy some bread.

"From Osmanieh, I traveled by carriage to Rajo and passed thousands of Armenians en route to Aleppo. They were going in ox-carts, on horseback, donkeys and on foot, the most of them children, women and old men. I spoke to several of these people, some of whom had been educated in the American Mission Schools. They told me that they had traveled for two months. They were without money and food and several expressed their wish that they could die rather than go on and endure the sufferings that they were undergoing. The people on the road were carrying with them practically all their household possessions and those who had no carts or animals were carrying them on their backs. It was not unusual to see a woman with a big pack wrapped up in a mattress and a little child a few months old on the top of the pack. They were mostly bareheaded, and their faces were swollen from the sun and exposure. Many had no shoes on, and some had their feet wrapped in old pieces of rags, which they had torn from their clothing.

"At Intily there was an encampment of about ten thousand and at Kadma a large encampment of one hundred and fifty thousand. At this place, adjacent to their encampment, were Turkish troops who exacted "backshish" from them before they would let them go on the road to Aleppo. Many who had no money had had to stay in this camp since their arrival there about two months before. I spoke with several Armenians here and they told me the same story of brutal treatment and robbery at the hands of the gendarmes in charge, as I had heard all along the road. They had to go at least half a mile for water from this encampment, and the condition of the camp was filthy.

"From Kadma on to Aleppo I witnessed the worst sights of the whole trip. Here the people began to play out in the intense heat and no water, and I passed several who were prostrate, actually dying of thirst. One woman whom I assisted was in a deplorable condition and unconscious from thirst and exhaustion, and farther on I saw two young girls who had become so exhausted that they had fallen on the road and lay with their already swollen faces exposed to the sun.

"The road for a great distance was being repaired and covered with cracked stones; on one side of the road was a footpath, but many of the Armenians were so dazed from fatigue and exposure that they did not see this footpath and were walking—many barefooted—on the cracked stones, their feet, as a result, bleeding.

"The destination of all these Armenians is Aleppo. Here they are kept crowded in all available vacant houses, khans, Armenian churches, courtyards and open lots. Their condition in Aleppo is beyond description. I personally visited several of the places where they were kept and found them starving and dying by the hundreds every day.

"In one vacant house, which I visited, I saw women and children and men all in the same room lying on the floor so close together that it was impossible to walk between them. Here they had been for months, those who had survived, and the condition of the floor was filthy.

"The British Consulate was filled with these exiles, and from this place the dead were removed almost every hour. Coffin-makers throughout the city were working late into the night, making rough boxes for the dead whose relatives or friends could afford to give them decent burial.

"Most of the dead were simply thrown into two-wheeled carts, which made daily rounds to all the places where the Armenians were concentrated. These carts were open at first but afterward covers were made for them.

"An Armenian physician whom I know and who is treating hundreds of these suffering Armenians who have become ill through exposure on the trip, hunger and thirst, told me that there are hundreds dying daily in Aleppo from starvation and the result of the brutal treatment and exposure that they have undergone on the journey from their native places.

"Many of these suffering Armenians refused alms, saying that the little money so obtained will only prolong their sufferings and they prefer to die. From Aleppo, those who are able to pay are sent by train to Damascus, those who have no money are sent over the road to the interior toward Deir-El-Zor.

"In Damascus I found conditions practically the same as in Aleppo; and here hundreds are dying every day. From Damascus, they are sent still farther south into the Hauran, where their fate is unknown. Several Turks, whom I interviewed, told me that the motive of this exile was to exterminate the race, and in no instance did I see any Moslem giving alms to Armenians, it being considered a criminal offence for any one to aid them.

"I remained in Damascus and Aleppo about a month, leaving for Smyrna on the twenty-sixth of October. All along the road I met thousands of these unfortunate exiles still coming into Aleppo. The sights I witnessed on this trip were more pitiful than those I had seen on my trip to Aleppo. There seems to be no end to the caravan which moves over the mountain ridge from Bozanti south; throughout the

Ancient Aqueduct Crossing Meles River at Smyrna.

day from sunrise to sunset, the road as far as one can see is crowded with these exiles. Just outside of Tarsus I saw a dead woman lying by the roadside and farther on passed two more dead women, one of whom was being carried by two gendarmes away from the roadside to be buried. Her legs and arms were so emaciated that the bones were nearly through her flesh and her face was swollen and purple from exposure. Farther along, I saw two gendarmes carrying a dead child between them away from the road where they had dug a grave. Many of these soldiers and gendarmes who follow the caravan have spades and as soon as an Armenian dies they take the corpse away from the roadside and bury it. The mornings were cold and many were dying from exposure. There are very few young men in these caravans, the majority are women and children, accompanied by a few old men over fifty years of age.

"At Bairamoglou, I talked with a woman who was demented from the sufferings she had undergone. She told me that her husband and father had both been killed before her eyes and that she had been forced for three days to walk without rest. She had with her two little children and all had been without bread for a day. I gave her some money, which she told me would be taken, in all probability, from her before the day was over. Turks and Kurds meet these caravans as they pass through the country and sell them food at exorbitant prices. I saw a small boy about seven years old riding on a donkey with his baby brother in his arms. They were all that was left of his family.

"Many of these people go without bread for days, and they become emaciated beyond description. I saw several fall from starvation, and only at certain places along this road is there water. Many die of thirst. Some of the Armenians, who can afford it, hire carriages. These are paid for in advance and the prices charged are exorbitant.

"At many places like Bozanti, for example, where there is an encampment of Turkish soldiers, there is not enough bread for these Armenians and only two hours from Bozanti I met a woman who was crying for bread. She told me that she had been in Bozanti for two days and was unable to obtain anything to eat, except what travelers like myself had given her. Many of the beasts of burden belonging to the Armenians die of starvation. It is not an unusual sight to see an Armenian removing a pack from the dead animal and putting it on his own shoulders. Many Armenians told me that although they were allowed to rest at night, they get no sleep because of the pangs of hunger and cold.

"These people walk throughout the whole day at a shuffling gait and for hours do not speak to one another. At one place where I stopped along the road for lunch I was surrounded by a crowd of little children, all crying for bread. Many of these little tots are obliged to walk barefooted along the road and many of them carry little packs on their backs. They are all emaciated, their clothes are in rags and their hair in a filthy condition. The filth has given rise to millions of flies and I saw several babies' faces and eyes covered with these insects, the mothers being too exhausted to brush them away.

"Diseases broke out in several places along the road, and in Aleppo several cases of typhus fever among the Armenians were reported when I left. Many families have been separated, the men being sent in one direction and the women and children in another. I saw one woman, who was with child, lying in the middle of the road crying, and over her stood a gendarme threatening her if she did not get up and walk. Many children are born along the way and most of these die as their mothers have no nourishment for them.

"None of these people have any idea where they are going or why they are being exiled. They go day after day along the road with the hope that they may somewhere reach a place where they may be allowed to rest. I saw several old men carrying on their backs the tools of their trade, probably with the hope that they may some day settle down somewhere. The road over the Taurus Mountains in places is most difficult and often times crude conveyances drawn by buffalos, oxen and milk-cows are unable to make the grade and are abandoned and overturned by the gendarmes into the ravine below. The animals are turned loose. I saw several carts, piled high with baggage on the top of which were many Armenians, break down and throw their occupants in the road. One of the drivers, who was a Turk, and who had collected an advance from the people whom he was driving, considered it a huge joke when one woman broke her leg from such a fall.

"There seems to be no cessation of the stream of these Armenians pouring down from the North, Angora and the region around the Black Sea. Their condition grows worse every day. The sights that I saw on my return trip were worse than those on my trip going, and now that the cold weather and winter rains are setting in, deaths are more numerous. Roads in some places are almost impassable."

Chapter 9

INFORMATION FROM OTHER SOURCES

I HAVE often been impressed with the hopelessness of making people who have not been eye-witnesses, comprehend the dreadful character of the massacres which were carried on by the Turks against the Christian population of the Orient. I have never been able to describe sights that I have witnessed in such manner as to make my listeners actually see and understand. It frequently happens that people, sitting in their comfortable houses, lay aside an article or book on the subject, with the remark: "We are fed up on Armenian atrocities."

Here is another strong point of the Turk's position: he has killed so many human beings and over so long a period of time that people are tired of hearing about it. He can, therefore, continue without interference.

In Doctor Elliott's *Beginning Again at Ararat,* gives the following story of a young girl, heard in the rescue home in Turkey, of which she was in charge:

"I was twelve years old, I was with my mother. They drove us with whips and we had no water. It was very hot and many of us died because there was no water. They drove us with whips, I do not know how many days and nights and weeks, until we came to the Arabian Desert. My sisters and the little baby died on the way. We went to a town, I do not know its name. The streets were full of dead, all cut to pieces. They drove us over them. I kept dreaming about that. We came to a place on the Desert, a hollow place in the sand, with hills all around it. There were thousands of us there, many, many thousands, all women and girl children. They herded us like sheep into the hollow. Then it was dark and we heard firing all around. We said, "The killing has begun." All night we waited for them, my mother and I, we waited for them to reach us. But they did not come, and in the morning, when we looked around, no one was killed. No one was killed at all. They had not been killing us. They had been signaling to the wild tribes that we were there. The Kurds came later in the morning, in the daylight; the Kurds and many other kinds of men from the Desert; they came over the hills and rode down and began killing us. All day long they were killing; you see, there were so many of us. All they did not think they could sell, they killed. They kept on killing all night and in the morning—in the morning they killed my mother."

This quotation is given because it condenses in a few vivid and convincing words the clearest description that has appeared anywhere of the character of the Turkish "deportations" of the Armenians. All the official documents and the testimony of a host of American, German and other eye-witnesses corroborate the accuracy of this picture.

In the report of the Military Mission to Armenia, commonly known as the "Harbord Mission," published by the American Association for International Conciliation, in June, 1920, is to be found the following passage:

"Meanwhile there have been organized official massacres of the Armenians ordered every few years since Abdul Hamid ascended the throne. In 1895, one hundred thousand perished. At Van, in 1908, and at Adana and elsewhere in Cilicia in 1909, over thirty thousand were murdered. The last and greatest of these tragedies was in 1915. Massacres and deportations were organized in the spring of 1915, under a definite system, the soldiers going from town to town. Young men were first summoned to the government building in each village and then marched out and killed. The women, the old men and the children were, after a few days, deported to what Talaat Pasha called "Agricultural Colonies," from the high, breeze-swept plateaus of Armenia to the malarial flats of the Euphrates and the burning sands of Syria and Arabia. The dead, from this wholesale attempt on the race, are variously estimated at from five hundred thousand to a million, the usual figure being about eight hundred thousand. Driven on foot under a hot sun, robbed of their clothing and such petty articles as they carried, prodded by bayonets if they lagged, starvation, typhus, and dysentery left thousands dead by the trail side, etc., etc."

I have in my possession another report of a credible European who witnessed the destruction of the Armenians at Aleppo and elsewhere, which gives many details similar to those found in the memorandum of Mr. Geddes, but I refrain from offering it here for fear of wearying the readers. In view of the difficulty of producing the testimony of eye-witnesses, and as this report has never been published, it is a valuable historical document. Enough has been said, however, to convince the reader that the extermination of the Christians of Turkey was an organized butchery, carried out on a great scale, and well under way before the Greeks were sent to Smyrna. We have seen it in operation in the days of Abdul Hamid, "the butcher," we have seen it more fully developed and better organized under Talaat and Enver, those statesmen of the "Constitution." We shall behold it carried out to its dire finish by Mustapha Khemal, the "George Washington" of Turkey.

This part of the story would not be complete if I passed over in silence the systematic extermination, and the satiating of all the lowest passions of man or beast which characterize Turkish massacres of the Greeks and Armenians of the Pontus. There have been, from time to time, descriptions of the massing of bands of these wretched people at different points on the shores of the Black Sea where they had arrived after long journeys on foot and indescribable hardships, and of the relief given them by American organizations. Often officers of these organizations, or American missionaries, have uttered cries of protest, which have caused a momentary feeling of wonder in the minds of the American people, or have passed unheeded. Yet the systematic massacre, deportation, plundering and violation that went on among the Christians of once prosperous region of the Black Sea is one darkest and foulest pages even in Turkish history.

The flourishing communities of Amasia, Cæsarea, Trebizonde, Chaldes, Rhodopolis, Colonia, centers of Greek civilization for many hundreds of years have been practically annihilated in a persistent campaign of massacre, hanging, deportation, fire and rape. The victims amount to hundreds of thousands, bringing the sum total of exterminated Armenians and Greeks in the whole of the old Roman province of Asia up to the grand total of one million, five hundred thousand. Thus has been created that "regenerated" Turkey, which has been compared in some quarters to Switzerland and the United States.

Chapter 10

THE GREEK LANDING AT SMYRNA
(May, 1919)

I RETURNED to Smyrna in 1919, shortly after the Greek army had landed in the city. As the Turkish plan of extermination was well under way before the arrival of the Greek troops, the Christian peasants had been driven out of the entire region with the exception of the city itself, and many had perished, their farms and villages being destroyed. They had scattered over the Greek islands and the continent, and at Saloniki, where the Greek government had constructed barracks to house them, there was a considerable settlement of them.

Much has been said of atrocities and massacres committed by the Greek troops at the time of their landing at Smyrna on May 15, 1919. In fact, the events that occurred on that and the few succeeding days have been magnified until they have taken on larger proportions in the public mind than the deliberate extermination of whole nations by the Turks, and no consideration seems to have been given to the prompt suppression of the disorders by the Greek authorities and the summary punishment of the principal offenders, several of them by death.

The facts of the case, as learned from American missionaries, business men and others of undoubted veracity, are as follows: The evening before the disembarkment there was a reunion of the Allied naval commanders and, according to one of those present, there was a discussion as to the plan under which this action ought to be carried out. My informant stated that the American commander was in favor of cooperating with the Greeks by policing the different sections of the city with Allied Marines, but that the Englishman advocated letting the Greeks "run the whole show" alone. This information is given second hand and its accuracy can not be vouched for, but it seems probable.

At any rate, the advice attributed to the American was practical, but could not be followed for evident reasons. We could not disembark because we were, as usual, "observing"; and there was such strong jealousy among the Allies regarding Asia Minor, that they could not go ashore either together or separately. This was the first indication of the lack of united support that ultimately caused the Greek disaster and the destruction of Smyrna.

The whole responsibility was therefore thrown upon the Greeks, who landed among a population, so far as the Turks were concerned, more insulted by their advent than the white citizens of Mobil would be if it were given over to a mandate of negro troops. To the Turk, the Hellene is not only a "dog of an unbeliever," but he is a former slave.

As the Greeks proceeded in the direction of the *Konak,* or Government House, situated in the Turkish quarter, they were sniped at. I was informed by numerous eye-witnesses, not natives of Smyrna, that the sniping grew into a fusillade.

The sanitary expert of the American hospital, situated in the region of the *Konak,* related to me the following incident: Hearing the sniping, he ran out into the yard of the hospital, fearing that if shots were discharged from there they might draw the Greek fire. He saw a Turk with a rifle up in a tree of the hospital yard. He pointed a revolver at him and told him to come down. The Turk obeyed. This informant was a native-born American citizen, not of Greek or Armenian extraction.

The Greeks took a number of prisoners whom they marched down the quay in the sight of the Allied and American battle-ships, making them hold up their hands. They are said to have stabbed several of their prisoners with bayonets in sight of the people in the houses and on the ships. There was no massacre, in the sense of a general killing of prisoners, but some few they did thus kill; this act appears murderous, contemptible and idiotic, and the Greeks may be left to explain it as best they may.

There was an uprising in the town, something in the nature of a riot, and some more Turks were killed. Various estimates have been given by Americans who were present as to the number killed, ranging from fifty to three hundred. The latter is a high estimate. There was also considerable looting, both in Smyrna and the outlying regions.

Speaking of this affair in a pamphlet entitled *The Great Powers and the Eastern Christians,*[*] William Pember Reeves says:

"So far as the persons killed in Smyrna were Turks, they numbered, I am told, seventy-six, killed partly by Greek soldiers and

[*]   Published by the Anglo-Hellenic League, No. 49.

partly by the town mob. About one hundred of other nationalities were killed also. The ring leaders in the business were executed by the Greek authorities and compensation paid to the families of the victims."

Where Mr. Reeves obtained his information is unknown to me, but it coincides with that which was given me by Americans who were present and who I saw a short time after the landing of the Greek troops. I was present in Smyrna when the ring-leaders in the disturbances of May second were condemned and shot.

It was here that the Greek governor-general displayed that resolution and marked ability, which characterized his entire regime at Smyrna. He suppressed the disturbances completely in a very short space of time and severely punished the evil-doers. Three of the ringleaders, Greeks, were taken out to a square beside the railroad connecting Boudja and Smyrna and publicly shot and buried where their graves could be seen by all the people passing between that popular summer resort and the main city. This trio had been previously tried by court-martial and sentence had been executed immediately.

Many others were tried and received lesser sentences. The populace was informed that Greeks disturbing the peace would be more severely punished than Turks, a policy which was carried out during the entire Hellenic administration and contributed no little to the unpopularity of the governor-general among the native Christian population.[*]

Mr. Sterghiades, the Greek governor-general, ordered all those who had loot in their possession to give it back immediately, under pain of heavy punishment, and specified a certain warehouse on the Rue Franque where it was to be delivered, and practically all the plunder was given up. All Turks who claimed to have been robbed

---

[*] In all seventy-four sentences were passed on those convicted of disturbing public order on the days immediately following the landing of the Greek military authorities: three of death; four of hard labor for life; two of hard labor for a term of years; twelve of long and fifty-three of shorter terms of imprisonment. Of the seventy-four sentenced, forty-eight were Greeks; thirteen Turks; twelve were Armenians and one a Jew. The three persons executed were Greeks, one of them a soldier.

were invited to present their claims to the government and these were accorded with so little question that numerous Turks profited immensely by presenting false or exaggerated demands. In addition, many Greek landed proprietors and prominent inhabitants of the smaller towns went out into the country and by haranguing the peasants and protecting the Turks, contributed greatly to the restoration of order in the rural regions.

Prominent among these was a certain Mr. Adamopolos, owner of a very large estate at Develikeuy, a village about thirty-five miles out of Smyrna, who proceeded there and compelled his peasants to restore sheep and other belongings, and threatened with dire punishment any Greek who should harm a Turk.

There was also a lawyer by the name of Athinogenis, who calmed an uprising of Greek villagers at Boudja by explaining to them the real meaning of the Greek landing. Mr. Athinogenis came to America in behalf of the autonomy of Asia Minor and created a good impression here.

To this list must be added a certain Mrs. Baltadzis, wife of a naturalized American citizen, who visited a farm owned by her near Smyrna and kept the peasants in order. Tranquility was soon restored, as much by the influence of the better-class Greeks as by the severe measures taken by the Hellenic civil administration. That it could be so restored was nothing less than a miracle when one considers the persecutions, which the Greeks had so recently suffered. Many of the Greek peasants had been robbed and abused by the very Turks whom they would now gladly get even with.

One incident will be sufficient to illustrate the sort of thing that was smarting in the memory of the Christian peasantry: A small farmer with a large family had planted a field of beans for food for his wife and children—beans being one of the principal articles of food for these people. A Turkish officer staked out his horse in this field, whereupon the farmer asked him if he might not put the animal in a grass plot, where was excellent pasturage. The reply was a horse-whipping, accompanied by abusive and contemptuous epithets in the presence of his family and the village, by the officer. This is a mild incident illustrative of the general conduct of the Turks toward the Christians. It is given because it came within my personal observation, and I knew the farmer, who was a very worthy and self-respecting man.

Great numbers of the Greeks had almost unforgettable insults and injuries smoldering in their hearts. Standing on the balcony of the Consulate, I have seen a Turkish cabman pass a Greek confrere and lash him with his whip, a cowardly act, because resistance on the part of the latter would have meant death and there was no one to whom he could have recourse for justice. In many cases the Greeks who took the Turks' sheep were only trying to get their own back, previously taken.

One sinister event occurred in a village not far from Smyrna, which will be understood in this country especially in the Southern States. A certain powerful Turk had made free with several Christian girls, and soon after the landing the fathers and brothers seized and hanged him. The virtue of their women is an extremely sensitive point with Greeks.

Mr. Sterghiades, the Hellenic high-commissioner, or governor-general, was a remarkable man in many ways. A Cretan, like Mr. Venizelos, he had been selected by the latter for the post, and a more difficult it would not be easy to imagine. Possessed of a strict sense of justice and a high ideal of duty, he lived as a hermit, accepting no invitations and never appearing in society. He wished, he informed me, to accept no favors and to form no ties, so that he might administer equal justice to all, high and low alike. It soon became known that when he issued an order he expected it to be obeyed.

On one occasion I was present at an important service in the Orthodox Cathedral, to which the representative of the various powers, as well as the principal Greek authorities had been invited. The high-commissioner had given the order that the service should be strictly religious and non-political. Unfortunately, Archbishop Chrysostom (he who was later murdered by the Turks) began to introduce some politics into his sermon, a thing which he was extremely prone to do. Sterghiades, who was standing near him, interrupted, saying: "But I told you I didn't want any of this." The archbishop flushed, choked, and breaking off his discourse abruptly, ended with, "In the name of the Father, Son and Holy Ghost, Amen," and stepped off the rostrum.

The high-commissioner was once on his way to a country village to officiate at the dedication of a school when one of his companions said: "Some ugly stories are told about the priest out there. He refused to say the prayers over the dead body of a poor woman's child, because she did not have the full amount of his fee, and it was buried without the rites of the church."

The high-commissioner made no reply to this and expressed no opinion. On his arrival at the village a delegation came down to meet him, including the mayor, the priest, etc. Upon being presented to the father, the high-commissioner slapped the latter soundly in the face, saying: "Wretch! I don't want to know you. You are a disgrace to the Church and to the Greek nation."

"But this isn't the same priest, Excellency," explained the bystanders. "This is a good man. We sent the other away."

"Give him a hundred drachmas for his poor," said His Excellency to his secretary, and thus the incident was closed. At any rate, he had forcibly expressed his opinion of the sort of man the guilty priest was.

Chapter 11

THE HELLENIC ADMINISTRATION
IN SMYRNA
(May 15, 1919–September 9, 1922)

DESPITE many difficulties, the Greek civil authorities, as far as their influence extended, succeeded in giving Smyrna and a large portion of the occupied territory, the most orderly, civilized and progressive administration that it has had in historic times. Mr. Sterghiadis, who continued to the last his policy of punishing severely all offenders of Greek origin against the public order, lost, for that reason, popularity in Asia Minor. When he left Smyrna after the debacle of his troops he was hooted by the people of the town who had not come loyally to his support. He was, indeed, a great man who made a supreme effort to perform a super-human task and who is suffering from the obloquy that always attaches to failure.

Here are some of the civilizing reforms which the Hellenic administration introduced into the Smyrna region:

1. During the war, under Turkish rule, the morality of the Christian inhabitants of all nationalities had greatly deteriorated. The Turk had no respect or regard for non-Mussulman women, whom he regards as his legitimate prey. All the American residents of Smyrna during this epoch will remember the orgies indulged in by a certain high Turkish official and his friends and the example set the European colony by a prominent Anglo-Levantine lady who became his acknowledged and public mistress. The lady in question was proud of her position and afterward explained it by saying that she had accepted it to use her influence to prevent persecutions and that a monument should be set up in her honor.

In one of the first conversations which I had with Mr. Sterghiades after his arrival, the governor general told me that the Christian people had been debauched by the Turks and had lost their self-respect and their morality, and that they needed an awakening of their pride of race and religious instincts. One of his first acts was to suppress the disorderly houses located in the central portions of the town, and in this he met with determined opposition from various of the foreign consuls whose subjects owned these houses and conducted them. Helpless to enforce an edict against a European subject, he stationed gendarmes in front of the establishments in question who took down the names and addresses of all frequenters and thus caused their patronage so to dwindle that they were obliged to close.

Playing of baccarat and other forms of gambling for high stakes had also become a crying evil in Smyrna, resulting in the ruin of several people and even in suicides. Mr. Sterghiades suppressed gambling in the clubs, and private houses, wherever it came to his notice.

2. The Hellenic Administration supported and aided in every way possible educational institutions. Its support and encouragement of American educational and philanthropic institutions will be taken up later. It is chiefly to be praised, however, for the measures which it took, paid for out of the Greek Treasury, for the maintenance and improvement of Turkish schools. It continued the Moslem secondary schools at its own expense, the taxes for their support having been taken over by the Ottoman public debt as security for a loan contracted by the Ottoman Government.

The Greek administration supported by funds from its treasury, two Moslem high schools in Smyrna, two at Magnesia and Odemish, and two seminaries in the provinces, paying therefore yearly seventy thousand Turkish pounds. It kept in vigor the Turkish system of primary education, appointing prominent Mussulmans in the various villages to superintend the same. It maintained a Polytechnic school at Smyrna, at which two hundred and ten poor Mussulman, children were educated and supported, paying therefore thirty-six thousand Turkish pounds yearly.

In addition to this, it was especially helpful to those American institutions and schools, which operated in the Turkish quarter and among Turkish children.

3. The Greek administration made a serious and intelligent effort to organize a sanitary service for the compiling of statistics, the betterment of sanitary conditions and the suppression of epidemics and contagious diseases, such as malaria, syphilis, etc.

A microbiological laboratory was established for the diagnosis of infectious diseases with an equipment of sanitary motorcars for

White Tower at Saloniki, formerly seaward terminal of ancient wall.

bringing in the sick from distant points, small wagons for the transportation of infected articles and portable outfits for disinfections on the spot. To describe the work of this service alone, which was organized on a large scale and abundantly supplied with means, material and money, would require a good-sized pamphlet. As a result of these measures, plague, exanthematic fever and smallpox were got so under control that they disappeared as epidemic diseases in the occupied zone. Needless to say that systematic war was waged against lice and rats.

A Pasteur institute was opened at Smyrna by the Greeks on the eighteenth of August, 1919, under the direction of a specialist working in conjunction with a staff of experts. Out of over one thousand five hundred patients treated during the first two months of its existence who had been bitten by dogs, jackals or wolves, only four died. Treatment was free in this institute. Previously sufferers had been obliged to go to Constantinople or Athens and those who could not raise the funds were left to die. I have myself assisted poor Turks, frantic with fear, to make the trip to Constantinople for treatment.

One section of the University of Smyrna, founded by the Greek administration, was that of the Institute of Hygiene, divided into two sections, hygiene and bacteriology. It was all ready for business when the Turks burned Smyrna, possessing an installation similar to that of the great universities of Europe, including a good library and complete equipment of appliances. It would never have lacked money or support, and would have been at the service of all classes, irrespective of creed or race.

Here is the program which it was about to put in operation:

Gratuitous bacteriological, hygienic and industrial examinations for all classes of the community.

The preparation and gratuitous distribution of all healing and diagnostic inoculations, serums, anti-toxins, anti-gonococcus, etc.

The sanitation of the town on an extensive scale, sewerage, watersupply, streets, etc.

Sanitary works for the combating of malaria, the draining of marshes, etc.

The combating of trachoma.

ombating of phthisis on a large scale, (dispensaries, ums, convalescent homes, special hospitals, sanitation of houses, etc.)

For infants: dispensaries, *gouttes de lait, crèches,* foundling homes, etc.

For children: various philanthropic institutions. For mothers: pre-natal pre-culture.

Education and training of doctors to compose the service of public health.

Training for midwives and nurses.

Organization of a registry office of births and deaths.

Organization of special medical statistical service.

4. Financial aid on a large scale was furnished, as was the distribution of flour, clothing, etc., to refugees caused by the Khemalist raids in the interior and the destruction in 1919 of the cities of Aidin and Nazli. Among those so succored were thousands of Turks.

5. All American missionaries, as well as educational and charitable workers in Smyrna and its hinterland during the Greek occupation, will verify the statement that the Hellenic administration showed itself most helpful and cooperative in many ways, aiding their labors among Turks as well as Christians.

Here is a list of certain benevolent acts toward these institutions:

The high-commissioner granted to the Y.M.C.A. a large house on the quay, one of the biggest and finest in Smyrna, for use as a "Soldiers' Home." He also helped its management in many ways by detaching Greek soldiers for its service.

An adequate building was also given to be used as a "Soldiers' Home" at Magnesia, where many facilities were afforded.

The civil department of the Y.M.C.A. was in need of an adequate building for its installation. The Greek authorities requisitioned a café belonging to a Greek for that purpose. It was still in operation at the time of the burning of the city.

The same Y.M.C.A. organized on a large estate near Smyrna an installation for the study of agriculture by young men. The Greek administration helped this organization by furnishing tents, blankets and other requisites from the quarter-master's department and a motor-car for transportation.

The Y.M.C.A. had also organized at Phocea, near Smyrna, a summer camp for boys. The Greek administration helped by furnishing lumber, a boat and other materials, and allowed the importation of a motor-car free of duty.

The Y.W.C.A., which was managed by Miss Nancy McFarland, was helped in many ways by the Greek administration in the form of considerable sums of money, lumber and supplies.

A branch of the girls' school, known as the Intercollegiate Institute, was started at Guez Tepe by Miss Minnie Mills for Mussulman women. The high-commissioner furnished a part of the equipment for this.

For the N. E. R. at Smyrna the high-commissioner gave Miss Harvey five hundred pounds Turkish to be used in favor of poor Mussulman women.

The American College near Smyrna is situated in a place contiguous to a marsh formerly flooded by stagnant water causing malaria. The Greek administration drained the swamp and repaired the road passing by the college.

All the agricultural implements, which were imported for the use of the returning Greek refugees or for resale at cost price or on credit for the purpose of restoring the destroyed areas were purchased by the high commission exclusively from American factories at my request. Thus thousands of plows were brought in to be distributed among Turks as well as Christians.

A farm of thirty thousand acres situated at Tepekeuy, used by the Greek administration for the study of motor-culture, was bought and made exclusive use of American motor-plows. As a result, students completing the course recommended to the landowners the use of American motor-plows.[*]

During the Greek administration, I traveled frequently over a large part of the occupied territory and visited many of the interior villages. I found perfect security everywhere, native Greeks and Turks living together on friendly terms. In general there would be in each village a small administrative office in charge of a petty officer and two or three aides. I noticed the persistent effort, which these people made to fraternize with the Turks and to placate them. Very often have I taken my coffee in the public square of some small town with the Greek officials, the Turkish hodja,[†] and various of the Mohammedan notables. I remember particularly shortly before the

Greek defeat sitting thus with a venerable hodja and a Greek surgeon under a plane-tree, helping to celebrate the marriage of the hodja to his fourth wife, which had taken place the day before.

The dark side of this seemingly idyllic picture is that quite frequently the two or three Greek officials would be found some morning with their throats cut, whereupon an order would be sent to the village that the names of the assassins must be revealed or the town would be burned. This, if I remember correctly, was modeled upon our so-called "punitive expeditions" in the Philippines, which the Greek authorities often cited to me in speaking of the matter. In no case did the Turks reveal the names of the offenders and at least twice my office has been invaded by the notables of some town who complained that their village had been burned. On each occasion, I asked: "Were the Greek officials in your town murdered last night?" And the answer on both these occasions was, "Yes, but we could not tell the names of the offenders because we did not know who they were."

There were also sporadic acts of great ferocity committed against the peaceful Christian inhabitants of the country, which were always attributed by the Turks to roving bands of Chetas. Who these Chetas were, I do not know, but it is my opinion that they did not come from far. I remember one particularly atrocious case—the massacre and disemboweling of a Greek miller and his wife and their two children.

---

* While I was in Saloniki during the war, the American Y.M.C.A. was greatly aided, both financially and morally, by the Greek authorities, both Mr. Venizelos and the Greek archbishop being friendly to this institution and present at the dedication of its new house.

The American missionaries, who had an agricultural college and a school there, were at first viewed with suspicion by the Greeks for the reason that they all spoke Bulgarian and continued to reach in that language after the Greek occupation. I brought the missionaries and the Greek authorities together and since then the said authorities have been most benevolent to the missionaries and helpful to them in many ways. At my invitation the late King Alexander came to Saloniki to visit the various missionary and educational institutions and assured them of his friendly interest and support.

† A teacher in the secondary Turkish school attached to a mosque.

Chapter 12

THE GREEK RETREAT
(1922)

FOR years the Greek army had been holding a long line without sufficient food and clothing. Many of these troops had been sent by the Allies to fight for them in Russia where they had suffered severe losses. They were reduced to a state of extreme demoralization. They were fleeing from an implacable enemy from whom they could expect no mercy, if captured. They covered, such of them as got away, the distance from the front to the coast in record time. The entire Moslem population through which they passed was hostile and well-armed. That they found time to do much massacring or that they were in a state of mind to stop by the way for the purpose of attacking women seems hardly credible. That they did burn and lay waste the land may be taken for granted. The Greeks have claimed military necessity for this, and it would appear that they could plead such necessity if ever it can be pleaded. They certainly had more reason for laying bare the country between themselves and the advancing Khemalists than had our own Sherman on his "March to the Sea."

There is one thing, which any one who has ever traveled through Turkish-ruled lands will see at a glance. Whatever nuclei of civilization existed in the Ottoman Empire outside of Constantinople were Greek, Armenian or something besides Turkish. The non-Mussulmans built the good houses and the better parts of the towns. Many of the Christian houses and towns had already been destroyed by the followers of Talaat and Enver, leaving little of any permanent value in the path of the Greek army.

A Turkish villager's house usually consists of one room without any furniture. At one side is piled, often as high as the wall, a supply of thick quilts. When he goes to bed he takes down one or more of these and sleeps on the floor, or, in the better houses, on a bench that runs around the wall. When he eats he sits on the floor with his heels under him. He cooks in the fireplace. His culinary outfit consists of one earthen pot, a large wash-basin out of which the family eats their *pilaff,* one big spoon for each member of the household and a small one for stirring the coffee. A *briki,* or long-handled coffee pot, is an important part of his installation.

Many who have dined with rich denatured Turks at Constantinople or with some pasha will deny the accuracy of this picture, but it is in the main correct and describes the houses that compose ninety-nine out of a hundred Turkish villages wherever found. It is for this reason that the Turk may be able to carry on for a long time without business, manufactures, imports or any of the accessories of civilization. His crude agriculture will suffice for his primitive wants. If the region which he occupies really belongs to him, then he may say that he has a right to the kind of civilization, or lack of it, that suits him best and for which he is most adapted. Whether the Christian world should have looked on and aided him while exterminating the non-Mussulman population of Asia Minor is another question.

The difficulties of the Greek retreat are well illustrated by an incident narrated to me by the Reverend Dana Getchell who came into my office from the interior a few days before the arrival of the Khemalists. He said that when he had gone to bed in the evening in his small hotel everything had been quiet, but that he had been awakened in the morning by the sound of tumult in the streets, and looking from the window, he saw the whole Christian population rushing toward the railroad station, carrying such of their belongings as they had been able to snatch. On inquiring what the trouble was he was informed that the Turks were coming. He went to the station himself and saw a long train of cars on to which a small detachment of Greek soldiers was attempting to embark the frightened people. While this operation was being conducted the Mussulman villagers came out from their houses, all armed, and began to fire upon the soldiers and the train. A battle ensued in which the officer commanding the detachment and several of his soldiers were killed. But the soldiers stood their ground well and succeeded finally in getting away with the larger part of the Christians.

This specific incident throws light upon the Greek retreat as it shows that the Moslems were, in general, in possession of concealed weapons and that they did not hesitate to use them.

Chapter 13

SMYRNA AS IT WAS

THE burning of Smyrna and the massacre and scattering of its inhabitants has aroused wide-spread humanitarian and religious interest on account of the unparalleled sufferings of the multitudes involved. But there is another element in the United States, not numerous, that has been more deeply saddened by the fate of this ancient town—the classical scholars and historians.

The eyes of scholars, ever since the great discoveries of Schliemann, have been turned toward the island of Crete, where it is now known that a highly developed civilization existed, contemporaneous with early Egyptian, and of which the ancient cities of Tyrins and Mycenae were outposts. It is believed that the ancestors of the royal houses of these settlements came originally from Asia Minor, and it is possible that the conception of the grim old lions above the gate of Mycenae, symbolizing the courage of its kings, may have been imported from Asia. Theseus, that attractive and romantic hero, who finally became one of the rulers of the Mythical Age of Athens, is connected with Asia Minor through the Amazons, who were feminine priestesses of the old cult of the many-breasted nature goddess of Ephesus.

From Ionia, the mother civilization spread to old Greece, to Sicily, to Italy and along the shores of the Black Sea, and finally to Europe and America! It is more than probable that Homer was a Smyrniote, or an inhabitant of Asia Minor, and for countless years his writings were a sort of Bible or sacred book, molding the character of millions. Perhaps the earliest conception of monogamy, certainly the most beautiful, comes from Homer's poems. Our conception of the family is Greek; we get it from the Odyssey, very probably written in Smyrna, thousands of years ago.

During the days of the Byzantine Empire, that splendid, romantic and tragic power which developed a magnificent civilization and kept the lamp of learning alight all through the darkness of the Middle Ages, Asia Minor flourished and was the province which contributed most to the strength and firmness of the general fabric. The exploits of Nikephoros Phokas and the romance of Diogenes Akritas, immortalized in verse, are well known even to those scholars who are not Byzantine specialists. Those were the days of the great land barons who kept regal state and whose forgotten history should be a vast treasure-house for romantic novelists. Later, Ionia is of intense interest to the whole Christian world. It is the land of the Seven Cities of the Revelation, of the Seven Churches and the wonderful mystical poem of St. John the Divine. Six of the candles went out in eternal darkness long ago, but that of Smyrna burned brightly until its destruction on the thirteenth of September, 1922, by the Turks of Mustapha Khemal and the death of the last of its great bishops whose martyrdom fitly ended its glorious Christian history.

Polycarp, the patron saint of Smyrna during the long years of its existence as a Christian city, was burned alive in an ancient stadium whose contour is still plainly visible, on February twenty-sixth, in the year A. D. 156; Chrysostom was tortured and torn in pieces by a Turkish mob in front of the military headquarters of the Khemalist forces in Smyrna on September ninth, A.D. 1922. In Asia Minor were held the great Christian assemblies: at Nicaea, Ephesus and Chalcedon, were born the Church fathers, St. Paul and the two Gregories. It was at Ephesus, near Smyrna, that St. Paul fought with beasts after the manner of men.

Greek civilization has again and again developed in Asia Minor to be crushed by Asiatic invasion. At its height it produced the immortal cities of Pergamus, Smyrna, Colophon, Philadelphia, Ephesus, Halicarnassus. The whole land was dotted with lesser towns adorned with schools of art and beautiful temples from many of which sprang famous philosophers and poets. Ionia is a graveyard of ancient Greek cities and marble villages toward which the interest of American scholars has been turning more and more. A pioneer in this field was J. R. Sitlington Sterrett, who has left an unforgettable name among American archeologists.

The climate of Smyrna resembles very much that of Southern California. Snow rarely, if ever, falls in winter, and during the summer the country is daily refreshed by a breeze from the sea, the *embates,* or, in the Smyrna dialect, the *imbat.*

The route to Smyrna from Athens lies between Euboea and Andros and between the islands of Chios and Mytilini, the ancient Lesbos, famous as the home of Sappho. It skirts the great promontory of Kharabournou and enters the Hermian Gulf. To the left is the ancient city of Phocea. A colony from Phocea founded Marseilles, France, some thousands of years ago. It is interesting to know that the massacre and expulsion of the inhabitants in June, 1914, excited special interest and sympathy in the modern French city.

The harbor of Smyrna is one of the best in the world, comparable to that of Vancouver. At the bottom of the Hermian Gulf we come to a sort of sea-gate, the entrance to the harbor proper, in which the largest sea-going craft can safely anchor. Smyrna has attained great importance in late years as a commercial port. While other harbors, especially that of its ancient rival, Ephesus, have been filled by deposits brought down by the rivers, that of Smyrna has not suffered the same fate, the silt of the delta of the Hermus having tended only to narrow its mouth.

Among the first objects pointed out to the traveler on entering the bay are the "Two Brothers," or twin mountain peaks, which are identical in appearance. At the right is the ancient fortress bombarded by the British fleet during the war whose guns can plainly be seen by passengers upon steamers. Soon after passing the fortress, Smyrna appears nestling in the arms of a long, white, semicircular bay, resembling that of Naples, to which it is scarcely second in beauty, and climbing the slopes of Mount Pagus, crowned by an ancient wall and fortress. The city itself, with its suburbs, stretched far around the semicircle on both sides.

At the time of its destruction it is probable that the inhabitants exceeded five hundred thousand in numbers. The latest official statistics give the figure as four hundred thousand, of whom one hundred and sixty-five thousand were Turks, one hundred and fifty thousand Greeks, twenty-five thousand Jews, twenty-five thousand Armenians, and twenty thousand foreigners: ten thousand Italians, three thousand French, two thousand British and three hundred Americans.

The principal promenade was the quay, on which were located the American theater, the prettiest building of its kind in the Ottoman Empire, many cinemas, the best hotels, various modern and well-constructed office buildings, besides the residences of the most prosperous merchants, among whom were Greeks, Armenians and Dutch. On this street also were several of the Consulates, the building owned by the French Government being an imposing structure, suitable even for an embassy.

The residences mentioned were elegant in appearance and contained treasures of rugs, expensive furniture, works of art and Oriental curios.

The city was divided largely into quarters, though this was not a rigid arrangement. The Turkish lay to the east and south, and, as is usual in all mixed Ottoman towns, occupied the highest part, extending up the sides of Mount Pagus, (and does still, for that matter, as it was not burned). Architecturally it is a typical jumble of ramshackle huts, with very few, if any, buildings of a superior order. To the east are grouped most of the Jews, while the Armenian quarter lay to the north of the Turkish and contiguous with it. The Greek area was north again of the Armenian.

In speaking of the population of Smyrna one should not forget to mention the "Levantines." There seems to be some doubt in the American mind as to who these really are. The term is usually applied to any inhabitant of the Near East, and is supposed to carry with it an implication of deceit and sharpness in business. A "Levantine" is really a foreigner whose forefathers settled in that country one or more generations ago, who has become thoroughly versed in Oriental dealings, who speaks the languages, and some of whose ancestors may have intermarried with Greeks or Armenians.

As the Oriental understands it, the population of that country consists of Turks, Greeks, Armenians, Jews and Levantines. The latter have thrived immensely, and there are two small towns, Boudja and Bournabat, both within half an hour by rail from the metropolis, inhabited principally by descendants of British, French and Dutch, whose ancestors settled a hundred years or so ago in the Near East. These two villages are very beautiful. Many of the residences are imposing, and the parks and rose gardens surrounding them are not surpassed anywhere in the world. Their owners lived, (or live, such of them as have gone back) the lives of merchant princes. They have been able, protected by the capitulations, to amass great fortunes. These people generally resent being called "Levantines," and cling to their original nationality. During the Great War their sons enlisted

Turkish public letter writer, at Smyrna, receiving dictation of illiterate but amorous maiden.

with enthusiasm, and the German and Turkish cannon and other instruments of destruction took heavy toll of the debonair and wealthy youth of Boudja and Bournabat.

The principal business thoroughfare of Smyrna was the Rue Franque, on which were situated the great department and wholesale stores of the Greeks, Armenians and Levantines. At the shopping hour in the afternoon, this street was so crowded that one moved through it with difficulty, and among the motley throng ladies in costumes of the latest fashion, looking for that sort of merchandise that ladies shop for everywhere, formed a large part.

Social life presented many attractions. Teas, dances, musical afternoons and evenings were given in the luxurious *salons* of the rich Armenians and Greeks. There were four large clubs: the *Cercle de Smyrne,* frequented mostly by British, French and Americans; the "Sporting" with a fine building and garden on the quay; the Greek Club and a Country Club near the American college with excellent golf links and race course.

In no city in the world did East and West mingle physically in so spectacular a manner as at Smyrna, while spiritually they always maintained the characteristics of oil and water. One of the common sights of the streets was the long camel caravans, the beasts passing in single file, attached to ropes and led by a driver on a donkey in red fez and rough white-woolen cloak. These caravans came in from the interior laden with sacks of figs, licorice root, raisins, wood, tobacco and rugs. While the foreigner is apt to be afraid of these ungainly beasts, one often saw a Greek or Armenian woman in high-heeled boots and elegant costume, stoop and lift the rope between two camels and pass under. At the north end of the city is a railroad station called "Caravan Bridge", because near by is an ancient stone bridge of that name over which the camel caravans arriving from as far away as Bagdad and Damascus, used to pass.

Reference has already been made to the gaiety of the natives. One of the chief institutions of Smyrna about which naval men always inquire, was the *Politakia,* or orchestras of stringed instruments, guitars, mandolins and zither. The players added great zest to the performance by singing to their own accompaniment native songs and improvisations. The various companies gave nightly concerts in the principal cafés and were often called upon for entertainments in private houses.

The lightheartedness of the Smyrniotes was well-nigh irrepressible and continued almost until the last days when it was extinguished forever. During the Great War the British bombarded the fortress. At first the sound of the big guns terrified the inhabitants, but when it was discovered that there was no intention of throwing shells into the city itself the whole population gathered on the house-tops and at the cafés to witness the flashes and the bursting of the projectiles. The cannonading was plainly visible from the quay and became a regular theatrical performance, chairs on the sidewalks being sold at high prices.

Passing from the European quarter—Greeks and Armenians are here classed as Europeans—into the Turkish, one found himself in the days of the *Arabian Nights*. The civilization, the manners, the isolation of the women, who were either not seen at all or passed through the streets closely veiled, were all such as one finds described in the *Thousand and One Nights*. Mention should be made particularly of the letter-writers, generally kindly old hodjas, who sat at tables taking down the love-letters and other missives that were whispered in their ears. Groups of befezzed Mussulmans sat about smoking their water pipes beside antique fountains or in the shade of clambering grape-vines.

The American interests in Smyrna were very important. Besides the omnipresent Standard Oil Company, there were the great McAndrews and Forbes licorice firm with its spacious offices and thousands of employees and laborers, all the principal tobacco companies whose business amounted to millions yearly, the exporters of figs and raisins and carpets, and after the Greek occupation, the importers of agricultural implements and automobiles.

There were important American educational and humanitarian institutions as well as archeological expeditions to Sardis and Colophon. The excavators at Sardis during their last campaign made a notable discovery of thirty gold coins of Croesus, which were taken charge of by me and brought to the United States immediately after the Smyrna disaster. They also, with my aid, succeeded in obtaining the first large consignment of original marbles that has ever been sent to any American museum. These latter were shipped to America for the Metropolitan Museum of New York. All these marbles and coins were, for political reasons, sent back to Constantinople from New York.

I shall permit myself to digress sufficiently at this point to make the observation that I took keener satisfaction in bringing these remarkable antiquities to the United States than in any other single act of my entire consular career. This satisfaction was shared by the late Howard Crosby Butler, who added to my pleasure by his unstinted commendation. Perhaps if this great scholar and courtly gentleman had not died suddenly in Paris, he might have prevented the sacrifice of these treasures to business and political interests— futilely and unreasonably sacrificed.

Among the interesting ancient monuments existing in Smyrna are two aqueducts, which can be seen from the railroad running to Boudja. There is also the so-called "Tomb of Tantalus," the mythical founder of the town. The excellent water supply of the city is still derived from an ancient source known as the "Baths of Diana."

The road from Smyrna to Boudja skirts the beautiful Valley of St. Anne, so named because she is supposed to have been buried there. Through this flows the river known as the Meles, by the banks of which Homer may have composed his great epics.

The civilization of this ancient and beautiful city was essentially Greek. The great mills of Nazli, which before the war supplied an excellent quality of flour not only to Smyrna vilayet, but to the rest of Turkey and even exported to Europe, were founded by a Greek. Of the three hundred and ninety-one factories at Smyrna, three hundred and forty-four were Greek and fourteen Turkish. Statistics of this nature could be multiplied indefinitely.

The two principal native schools—both Greek—were the Homerion, an institution for girls, and the Evangelical School for Boys, the latter under British protection. These were academies of great merit, affording a liberal course of education, and their graduates, many of them successful men and women, are to be found in all parts of the world. The library of the Evangelical School was recognized by scholars as containing a large and invaluable collection of books, manuscripts and inscriptions, many of which can never be replaced.

Among other irreparable losses caused by the fire should be mentioned two very ancient copies of the Bible, one kept in a church in Smyrna, and the other the special charge of a small community of Christians who are said to have fled from Ephesus when that city was sacked by the Turks centuries ago, and to have founded a small village whose sole object was the preservation of this venerable book. This part of the tale should not be finished without reference to the records of the American Consulate. Smyrna was one of the oldest of our foreign offices and contained many dispatches signed by Daniel Webster and others equally famous in our history, besides interesting references to incursions of the Barbary pirates, and an account of the saving of a famous Polish patriot by a small American cruiser, which cleared for action and demanded his release from an Austrian battle-ship. There have been many thrilling and inspiring episodes in the history of our navy where commanders have acted on their own responsibility in behalf of justice and humanity. Such episodes were more frequent before the perfection of the wireless and the submarine telegraph. It is a consolation to reflect that the spirited incident mentioned above occurred in the harbor of Smyrna, to balance, as it were, the history of the locality.

I was engaged before the fire in going through the ancient records and preparing a resume of their contents. Among the treasures of the Consulate were twelve magnificent old wood-prints of the battle of Navarino, giving different stages of the action, with faithful reproductions of the various ships with their names, which, as they were my personal property, I had intended to present to our navy department. I believe that there are no other copies of these prints in existence.

Smyrna is now a mass of ruins and a Turkish village. It should be borne in mind, however, that history repeats itself. Smyrna was rebuilt by Greeks after its destruction by Lydians, and Hellenic civilization again reasserted itself after the ferocity of the Turkish pirates of 1084, and the frightful butcheries of Tamerlane. A great city is the flower of industry and a peaceful and prosperous civilization. When the farmers swarm over the plains and the sailors go down to the sea in ships, then the bazaars and warehouses are built, the banks and the counting-houses and the shops of the cunning artisans. Smyrna will grow great again when a live and progressive Western civilization once more develops in Ionia. History has demonstrated that the Greeks, from their geographical position, their industrial and economic enterprise, and their relative maritime supremacy in the Mediterranean are the people ultimately destined to carry European progress into Asia Minor unless, indeed, Christianity should utterly fail, and with it, the civilization founded upon it.

Smyrna is too near Europe for Turkish retrogression and blight to rest there indefinitely. Its fields are too rich and too valuable to the human race to remain permanently in the hands of a sparse population of incompetent shepherds. The question is often asked: "When will the Turks rebuild Smyrna?" Turkish Smyrna was not burned.

Chapter 14

THE DESTRUCTION OF SMYRNA
(September, 1922)

THE last act in the fearful drama of the extermination of Christianity in the Byzantine Empire was the burning of Smyrna by the troops of Mustapha Khemal. The murder of the Armenian race had been practically consummated during the years 1915–1916, and the prosperous and populous Greek colonies, with the exception of Smyrna itself, had been ferociously destroyed. The idea has been widely circulated, and seems to be gaining credence, that the Turk has changed his nature overnight.

The destruction of Smyrna happened, however, in 1922, and no act ever perpetrated by the Turkish race in all its bloodstained history, has been characterized by more brutal and lustful features, nor more productive of the worst forms of human sufferings inflicted on the defenseless and unarmed. It was a fittingly lurid and Satanic finale to the whole dreadful tragedy. The uncertainty which at one time existed in the public mind as to the question, "Who burned Smyrna?", seems to be pretty well dispelled. All statements that tend to throw doubt on the matter can be traced to suspicious and interested sources. The careful and impartial historian, William Stearns Davis, to whom reference has already been made in this work, says: "The Turks drove straight onward to Smyrna, which they took (September 9, 1922) and then burned."[*]

Also, Sir Valentine Chirol, Harris Foundation lecturer at the University of Chicago in 1924, made this statement: "After the Turks had smashed the Greek armies they turned the essentially Greek city (Smyrna) into an ash heap as proof of their victory."[†]

Men of this stamp do not make assertions without having first gone carefully into the evidence.

We have already seen by what methods the Greeks had been eliminated from the coastal region of Asia Minor. The murders and

---

[*]   *A Short History of the Near East,* page 393.
[†]   *The Occident and the Orient,* page 58.

deportations have been described by which a flourishing and rapidly growing civilization had been destroyed, villages and farmhouses wrecked and vineyards uprooted. Large numbers of Greeks, however, who had managed to escape by sea, returned to their ruined homes after the landing of the Hellenic army in May of 1919, and set to work industriously to restore their ruined properties.

Mustapha Khemal now determined to make a complete and irretrievable ruin of Christianity in Asia Minor. *Carthago delenda est.* The plan, revealed by its execution, was to give the city up for some days to lust and carnage; to butcher the Armenians, a task which has always given a special pleasure to the Turk; to burn the town and to carry the Greek men away into captivity.

The main facts in regard to the Smyrna fire are:

1. The streets leading into the Armenian quarter were guarded by Turkish soldier sentinels and no one was permitted to enter while the massacre was going on.

2. Armed Turks, including many soldiers, entered the quarter thus guarded and went through it looting, massacring and destroying. They made a systematic and horrible "clean up," after which they set fire to it in various places by carrying tins of petroleum or other combustibles into the houses or by saturating bundles of rags in petroleum and throwing these bundles in through the windows.

3. They planted small bombs under the paving stones in various places in the European part of the city to explode and act as a supplementary agent in the work of destruction caused by the burning petroleum which Turkish soldiers sprinkled about the streets. The petroleum spread the fire and led it through the European quarter and the bombs shook down the tottering walls. One such bomb was planted near the American Girls' School and another near the American Consulate.

4. They set fire to the Armenian quarter on the thirteenth of September 1922. The last Greek soldiers had passed through Smyrna on the evening of the eighth, that is to say, the Turks had been in full, complete and undisputed possession of the city for five days before the fire broke out and for much of this time they had kept the Armenian quarter cut off by military control while conducting a systematic and thorough massacre. If any Armenians were still living in the localities at the time the fires were lighted they were hiding in cellars too terrified to move, for the whole town was overrun by

Turkish soldiers, especially the places where the fires were started. In general, all the Christians of the city were keeping to their houses in a state of extreme and justifiable terror for themselves and their families, for the Turks had been in possession of the city for five days, during which time they had been looting, raping and killing. It was the burning of the houses of the Christians, which drove them into the streets and caused the fearful scenes of suffering which will be described later. Of this state of affairs, I was an eye-witness.

5. The fire was lighted at the edge of the Armenian quarter at a time when a strong wind was blowing toward the Christian section and away from the Turkish. The Turkish quarter was not in any way involved in the catastrophe and during all the abominable scenes that followed and all the indescribable sufferings of the Christians, the Mohammedan quarter was lighted up and gay with dancing, singing and joyous celebration.

6. Turkish soldiers led the fire down into the well-built modern Greek and European section of Smyrna by soaking the narrow streets with petroleum or other highly inflammable matter. They poured petroleum in front of the American Consulate with no other possible purpose than to communicate the fire to that building at a time when C. Claflin Davis, Chairman of the Disaster Relief Committee of the Red Cross, Constantinople Chapter, and others, were standing in the door. Mr. Davis went out and put his hands in the mud thus created and it smelled like petroleum and gasoline mixed. The soldiers seen by Mr. Davis and the others had started from the quay and were proceeding toward the fire.

7. Dr. Alexander MacLachlan, President of the American College, and a sergeant of American Marines were stripped, the one of his clothes and the other of a portion of his uniform, and beaten with clubs by Turkish soldiers. A squad of American Marines was fired on.

Chapter 15

FIRST DISQUIETING RUMORS

MY wife and I were at Sevdikeuy, a Greek village a few miles south of Smyrna on the Ottoman railway, when the news that the Greek army was meeting with serious reverses arrived. These rumors were not believed at first, but they grew more and more insistent, throwing the population into an agony of fear.

At last the report became a certainty. The official news was received that the Greek army had suffered a terrible and irretrievable defeat and that nothing now prevented the Turks from descending to the coast. The population began to leave, a few at first, then more and more until the flight developed into a veritable panic.

The town was fast filling with refugees from the interior. The majority of these refugees were small farmers who had lived on properties that had descended from father to son for many generations. Their forebears had settled in Asia Minor before the Turks had begun to develop into a nation. They were children of the soil, able to live and care for themselves in their little houses and on their few acres, each family with its cow, its donkey and its goat. They were even producing tobacco, figs, seedless raisins and other products for export. They were expert in the cultivation and manipulation of the better qualities of cigarette tobacco and the priceless raisins, of which latter Asia Minor produces the best quality in the world. This valuable farmer element, the very backbone of the prosperity of Asia Minor, had again been reduced to beggary and thrown upon American charity. They were arriving by thousands in Smyrna and all along the seacoast. They were filling all the churches, schools and the yards of the Y. M. and Y.W.C.A. and the American mission schools. They were sleeping in the streets. Many were getting away during those first days on steamers and sailing craft. The *caiques* in the harbor, loaded with refugees and their effects, were a picturesque sight. For the man whose heart has not suffered atrophy as a result of the Great War, the spectacle of great numbers of helpless little children was particularly moving. Unfortunately, atrophy of the human heart has been one of the most noticeable phenomena of the great Armageddon. Doctor Esther Lovejoy, of New York, already referred to, used an expression with regard to certain Americans, who were present during the scenes of suffering and outrage.

"Their minds did not seem to register." Had she said "hearts," she would have been nearer the truth. The refugees carried with them as much of their belongings as their strength permitted and one often saw a little child sitting on top of a great bundle of bedding, the whole supported on the shoulders of some man or woman stumbling along.

In normal times the sick are not seen, as they are in the houses lying in bed for the most part. In case of a great fire or panic one is surprised at the number of sick or disabled thus brought to light. Many of the refugees were carrying sick upon their shoulders. I remember especially one old gray-haired woman stumbling through the streets of Smyrna with an emaciated feverish son astride her neck. He was taller than the mother, his legs almost touching the ground.

Then the defeated, dusty, ragged Greek soldiers began to arrive, looking straight ahead, like men walking in their sleep. Great numbers—the more fortunate—were sitting on ancient Assyrian carts, descendants of the very primitive vehicles used in the time of Nebuchadnezzar.

In a never-ending stream they poured through the town toward the point on the coast to which the Greek fleet had withdrawn. Silently as ghosts they went, looking neither to the right nor the left. From time to time some soldier, his strength entirely spent, collapsed on the sidewalk or by a door. It was said that many of these were taken into houses and given civilian clothes and that thus some escaped. It was credibly reported that others whose strength failed them before they got into the city were found a few hours later with their throats cut. And now at last we heard that the Turks were moving on the town. There had been predictions that Greek troops, on entering Smyrna, would burn it, but their conduct soon dispelled all such apprehensions. In fact the American, with the British, French and Italian delegates had called upon General Hadjianesti, the Greek commander-in-chief, to ask him what measures he could take to prevent acts of violence on the part of the disorganized Greek forces. He talked of a well-disciplined regiment from Thrace, which he was expecting and which he promised to throw out as a screen to prevent straggling bands from entering the city and even of organizing a new

resistance to the Turks, but could give the delegates no definite
assurance. He was tall and thin, straight as a ramrod, extremely well-
groomed, with a pointed gray beard and the general air of an
aristocrat. He was a handsome man, with the reputation of a lady-
killer. That was the last time I saw him, but when I read later of his
standing before a firing squad in Athens, I still retained a vivid mental
picture of that last interview in the military headquarters in Smyrna.
If it was he who was responsible for sending away the flower of his
troops to threaten Constantinople at a time when they were most
needed in Asia Minor, he deserved severe punishment or
confinement in a lunatic asylum. He had the general reputation of
being megalomaniac, with not too great ability. Certainly none but a
fool would have accepted the Smyrna post at that time for the sake of
glory. What was needed was a man of energy with a clear
understanding of the situation who would have taken hurried and
wise measures to save as much as possible of the wreckage. But
Hadjianesti was busy furnishing in gorgeous style and repairing a
palace on the quay, which he had requisitioned for a residence. He
deserved to be pitied, for it is probable that he was not well-balanced
mentally.

It was definitely asserted that the Turkish cavalry would enter the
town on the morning of September 9, (1922). The Greek general
staff and the high-commissioner with the entire civil administration,
were preparing to leave. The Greek gendarmes were still patrolling
the streets and keeping order. These men had gained the confidence
of every one in Smyrna and the entire occupied region by their
general efficiency and good conduct. Whatever accusations may be
substantiated against the Greek soldiers, nothing but praise can be
said of the Greek gendarmes. All my former colleagues at Smyrna and
all residents of the district will bear me out in this statement. There
would be an interval between the evacuation of Smyrna and the
arrival of the Turkish forces when the town would be without a
government of any kind. Some of the representatives of foreign
governments went to the high-commissioner and asked him to leave
the gendarmes until the Turks had taken over, under assurance from
the latter that they would be allowed to depart without molestation.
The high-commissioner did not grant this request. I did not join in
it. The Greek officials all left. Mr. Sterghiades had but a few steps to
go from his house to the sea where a ship was awaiting him, but he

was hooted by the population. He had done his best to make good in an impossible situation. He had tried by every means in his power to make friends of the implacable Turks, and he had punished severely, sometimes with death, Greeks guilty of crimes against Turks. He founded a university at Smyrna, bringing from Germany a Greek professor with an international reputation to act as president.

One of the last Greeks I saw on the streets of Smyrna before the entry of the Turks, was Professor Karatheodoris, president of the doomed university. With him departed the incarnation of Greek genius of culture and civilization in the Orient.

The Hellenic forces left, civil and military, and the interregnum of a city without a government began. But nothing happened. Mohammedans and Christians were quiet, waiting with a great anxiety. The supreme question was: How would the Turks behave? The French and Italian delegates assured their colonies that Khemal's army consisted of well-disciplined troops and that there was nothing to fear. I had no anxiety for the native-born Americans, but was very uneasy about the two hundred or more naturalized citizens, many of them former Ottoman subjects. I, therefore, did not take the responsibility of assuring the native population, Greeks and Armenians, that they would be perfectly safe, neither did I say anything that might tend to create panic. Many ladies, American and others, left at this time. I counseled my wife to go, but she refused, thinking that her staying might give comfort to those who remained. I decided to select a place of rendezvous for the American citizens and to notify all of them to keep in the neighborhood of this place as much as possible and, in case of serious disorders and general danger, to take refuge there. I picked out the American theater, a large and suitable building on the quay, for the purpose and called the leading members of the American colony, native and naturalized, to a meeting in my office and advised them of the measures taken, to be applied in case of need. When I told them that the meeting was dismissed, Mr. Rufus W. Lane, now a merchant of Smyrna, but formerly American consul there, arose and said: "We did not come here solely to save our own skins. The refugees that are pouring by thousands and thousands into the city are dying of starvation and nobody to help them. I had hoped that this meeting had been called together to take measures to succor these poor people." A Provisional Relief Committee was organized on the spot and a sufficient sum of money contributed to begin operations. All the leading American firms offered their lorries and automobiles and their personal services. Bakers were hired and set to work, stocks of flour found and purchased, and in a few hours this organization was feeding the helpless and bewildered refugees who were crowding into the city. But for the American colony in Smyrna thousands would have died of starvation before the Relief Unit could arrive from Constantinople.

In the meantime I was insistently telegraphing for American men-of-war to come to Smyrna. If there was ever a time when a situation demanded the presence of naval units, this, I thought, was that occasion. Though our colony was not great, our business interests and property holdings were very considerable indeed, to say nothing of our large schools with their staffs of teachers and professors.

The navy in those waters was under the control of that very fine officer and gentleman, Admiral Mark L. Bristol. I had reason to think that the admiral had perfect confidence in the good intentions and administrative abilities of the Turks and believed that the latter would bring a kind and benevolent administration to Smyrna. In response to telegraphic insistence with the State Department a wire was received to the effect that destroyers would be sent to Smyrna, as cruisers were not available, for the protection of American lives and property. Two small destroyers were accordingly sent. Naval units of Great Britain, Italy, France and the United States were present at Smyrna, and anchored but a few hundred yards or nearer from the houses on the quay during the appalling, shameful and heartrending scenes which followed

Chapter 16

THE TURKS ARRIVE

ON the morning of the ninth of September, 1922, about eleven o'clock, frightened screams were heard. Stepping to the door of my office, I found that a crowd of refugees, mostly women, were rushing in terror upon the Consulate and trying to seek refuge within, and that they were very properly being kept out by the two or three bluejackets assigned for the defense of the consular property.

One glance from the terrace which overlooked the quay made evident the cause of their terror. The Turkish cavalry were filing along the quay, on their way to their barracks at the *Konak* at the other end of the city. They were sturdy-looking fellows passing by in perfect order. They appeared to be well-fed and fresh. Many of them were of that Mongolian type which one sees among the Mohammedans of Asia Minor.

From the fact that not all the troops of Mustapha Khemal were provided with the smart uniforms of his picked troops, much has been made by Turkish apologists of the difference between "regulars" and "irregulars". Any one who saw those mounted troops passing along the quay of Smyrna would testify, if he knew anything at all of military matters, that they were not only soldiers, but very good soldiers indeed, thoroughly trained and under perfect control of admirable officers. And any one who knows anything of Turkish character will testify that the Turk is essentially a soldier, extraordinarily amenable to the orders of his superiors. The Turk massacres when he has orders from headquarters and desists on the second when commanded by the same authority to stop. Mustapha Khemal was worshipped by that army of "regulars" and "irregulars" and his word was law.

As the Turkish cavalry was entering Smyrna on the morning of the ninth, some fool threw a bomb. The Turkish officer commanding the cavalry division received bloody cuts about the head. All the testimony is to the effect that he rode unconcernedly on. That is what a Turk would do, for of the courage of the race there is

no doubt. It has been stated that this bomb was thrown by an
Armenian, but I have seen no proof of the assertion, nor can the
statement that the throwing of this bomb precipitated the massacre
of the Armenians, be reconciled with the Turkish claim that their
troops were so exasperated with the atrocities of the Greek army that
they could not be restrained when reaching Smyrna. Armenians are
not Greeks, and the fury of the Turks burst first upon their usual
victims.

On the evening of the ninth, the looting and killing began.
Shooting was heard in various parts of the town all night, and the
following morning native-born Americans, both men and women,
began to report seeing corpses lying about in the streets in the interior
of the town. Nureddin Pasha, the Turkish commander-in-chief,
issued a command that everybody was to go peacefully about his
business and that order should be preserved. This caused a
momentary feeling of security among a certain element of the non-
Mussulman population, so that a number of shops that had been
closed were reopened.

But this confidence was not of long duration, for the looting
spread and the savagery increased. At first, civilian Turks, natives of
the town, were the chief offenders. I myself saw such civilians armed
with shotguns watching the windows of Christian houses ready to
shoot at any head that might appear. These had the air of hunters
crouching and stalking their prey. But the thing that made an
unforgettable impression was the expression on their faces. It was that
of an ecstasy of hate and savagery. There was in it, too, a religious
exaltation, but it was not beautiful, it was the religion of the Powers
of Darkness. One saw, too, all the futility of missionary work and
efforts of conversion. Here was complete conviction, the absolute
triumph of error and the doctrine of murder and pitilessness. There
was something infinitely sad in those pale writhing faces on which
seemed to shine the wan light of hell. One could not help pitying
those men even while they were killing. One thought of lost souls and
the torments of the damned. Those killers were unhappy.

The last Greek soldiers disappeared from Smyrna on the evening
of the eighth and the Turks rapidly took over the town. Mounted
patrols and little squads of soldiers began to appear on the streets,
serving as police.

These were well enough behaved. There were credibly reported instances of minor Turkish officers interfering with the looters and evil-doers, and even of instances of kindness being shown to non-Mussulman natives. I saw no such kindness, however. If I had, I should be eager to report it, but I am willing to accept the testimony of others. The panic among the native Christians was now increasing to an alarming extent.

As the looting spread and the killing increased the American institutions were filled with frightened people. These institutions in Smyrna were the Intercollegiate Institute, a seminary for young girls; the Y.W.C.A., housed in a large building and surrounded by a garden and tennis court, and the Y.M.C.A.

The night of the tenth the shooting could still be heard in the Christian quarters and frightened people were besieging the doors of these institutions and screaming and begging in God's name to be let in. A number of bluejackets were stationed in both the girls' school and the Y.W.C.A., and if any of them chance to read these lines they will confirm the statement that the conduct of the American women teachers connected with the American institutions in and about Smyrna was without exception, above praise. There was not one who showed the least indication of fear or nervousness under the most trying circumstances; not one who flinched or wobbled for an instant throughout a situation which had scarcely a parallel in the history of the world for hideousness and danger. They endured fatigue almost beyond human endurance, that they might do all in their power to save their charges and give comfort and courage to the frightened hunted creatures who had thrown themselves on their protection. Such women as these throw imperishable luster on the name of American womanhood. Since none of them gave up or showed the white feather, we may conclude that they were worthy representatives of a worthy sisterhoood—the American Woman. For the men nothing need be said, for American men are expected to come up to the mark. I was proud of my whole colony at Smyrna.

Mention should be made of Jacobs, director of the Y.M.C.A. He was and is still, doubtless, famous for a genial smile which he himself calls the "Y.M.C.A. smile." Proceeding along the quay on an errand of mercy in connection with the refugees, he was stopped by several Turkish soldiers, searched and robbed of a sum of money.

Continuing his route, he hailed a Turkish officer to whom he complained. The officer asked him:

"Did they take it all?"

"Fortunately, no," replied Jacobs.

"Well then," said the officer, "hand over what you have left," which Jacobs was compelled to do. As he left he was shot at, but fortunately not hit. This incident I did not see, but it was related to me by other Americans.

The Turks were now making a thorough and systematic job of killing Armenian men. The squads of soldiers which had given the inhabitants a certain amount of comfort, inspiring the belief that the regular army was beginning to function and would protect the citizens, were chiefly engaged in hunting down and killing Armenians. Some were dispatched on the spot while others were led out into the country in squads and shot, the bodies being left in piles where they fell. The Americans belonging to the various charitable institutions, whose duties took them into the interior of the town, reported an increasing number of dead and dying in the streets.

A native-born American reported that he had seen a man beaten to death with clubs by the Turks, "till there was not a whole bone left in his body." The unwillingness of all the eye-witnesses to say anything that might offend the Turks and thus compromise their interests, shows how difficult it has been to get the full extent of the hideous and shameful truth.

Another native-born American, representative of a well-known tobacco firm, came white and trembling into the Consulate and reported that he had seen a terrible sight, "just around the corner." A number of Turkish soldiers had stopped an old man and commenced talking to him. The old man had thrown up his hands, the fingers spread in an attitude of supplication, whereupon one of the soldiers had split his hands with a sword, cut off his wrists and hewn him down.

The loot was now being driven out of the bazaars and the Armenian quarter by the cartload, and cartloads of corpses, as of beef or sheep, were being sent into the country.

The following is found in my memoranda dated September 12, 1922: "A party of Americans saw nine cartloads of dead bodies being carried off in the neighborhood of the *Konak* (Turkish government house) and another party saw three such cart-loads in the neighborhood of the Point Station."

Captain Hepburn, one of the naval officers, counted thirty-five dead bodies on the road leading to Paradise, a small village near Smyrna, where the American International College is situated.

At Boudja, another village, largely inhabited by English and other foreigners, there was a well-known and wealthy Dutch family by the name of De Jong. It was reported that Mr. and Mrs. De Jong had been murdered by Turkish soldiers. Concerning this affair, the following details were furnished me by Mr. Francis Blackler, one of the prominent members of the American community at Smyrna, head of the well-known firm of Griffith and Company, that does an extensive business with America. Mr. Blackler may be mentioned as neither he nor his wife, a lady of exceptional culture and refinement, has any idea of returning to Smyrna, at least under present conditions.

"I believe I was the first," he said, "to find and recognize the bodies of the De Jongs. I was passing along the street after the Turkish cavalry had passed through and I saw two bodies lying on the road. I stooped down and looked and immediately exclaimed, 'Why, that's Mr. De Jong!' Glancing at the other, I saw that it was Mrs. De Jong. The bodies were perforated with bullet holes. I notified the relatives and we took them away and buried them."

About this time, Sir Harry Lamb, the distinguished and able British consul-general, came to me and asked if I could send two automobiles to Bournabat to get Doctor Murphy and the women of his family. Besides my own car, there were quite a number of autos at my disposal, as the Americans of Smyrna owned many, practically all of which they had put at the disposition of the Consulate and the Relief Organization.

Doctor Murphy was a retired army surgeon who had been in the British Indian service. He was living with his two daughters on pension at Bournabat, an aged man with a high record. Sir Harry related that Turks had entered the Murphy home and told the doctor not to be frightened, as they meant harm to no one. They had simply come to violate the women. His daughters, fortunately, had hidden themselves in a room upstairs, but the eyes of the Turks fell upon a young and pretty servant. They attempted to seize her, when she fell on her knees and threw her arms about the legs of the aged doctor and begged him to save her. The old hero tried to protect the girl in so far as his feeble strength would allow, but he was beaten over the head with muskets, kicked, and the girl torn from him by the Turks. They then proceeded to accomplish their foul purpose. Sir Harry added that the doctor was in a desperate state and the women nearly dying from fright. The automobiles were sent and the Murphys brought down. The doctor died of his injuries.

The Archbishop Chrysostom came to the Consulate but a short time before his death, together with the Armenian Archbishop. Chrysostom was dressed in black. His face was pale. This is the last time that I saw this venerable and eloquent man alive. He was a constant friend of Americans and American institutions and used all his influence with the clergy and the government in favor of the support of our schools, our Y.W.C.A. and Y.M.C.A. It is doubtful if there is any member of our foreign missionary, educational and philanthropic institutions who will dispute this statement. He frequented them all and often addressed their members.

As he sat there in the consular office, the shadow of his approaching death lay upon his features. Some who read these lines—some few, perhaps—will understand what is meant. At least twice in my life I have seen that shadow upon a human visage and have known that the person was soon to die.

Monseigneur Chrysostom believed in the union of Christian churches, in a united effort in the cause of Christ and the better education of the Eastern clergy. Neither he nor the Armenian bishop spoke to me of their own danger, but they asked me if nothing could be done to save the inhabitants of Smyrna.

The tales vary as to the manner of Chrysostom's death, but the evidence is conclusive that he met his end at the hands of the Ottoman populace. A Turkish officer and two soldiers went to the offices of the cathedral and took him to Nureddin Pasha, the Turkish commander-in-chief, who is said to have adopted the medieval plan of turning him over to the fanatical mob to work its will upon him. There is not sufficient proof of the veracity of this statement, but it is certain that he was killed by the mob. He was spat upon, his beard torn out by the roots, beaten, stabbed to death and then dragged about the streets.

His only sin was that he was a patriotic and eloquent Greek who believed in the expansion of his race and worked to that end. He was offered a refuge in the French Consulate and an escort by French Marines, but he refused, saying that it was his duty to remain with his flock. He said to me: "I am a shepherd and must stay with my flock." He died a martyr and deserves the highest honors in the bestowal of the Greek church and government. He merits the respect of all men and women to whom courage in the face of horrible death makes an appeal.

Polycarp, the patron saint of Smyrna, was burned to death in the stadium overlooking the town. The Turk roams over the land of the Seven Cities and there is none to say him nay, but the last scene in the final extinction of Christianity was glorified by the heroic death of the last Christian bishop.

Looking from the door of the Consulate, I saw a number of miserable refugees with their children, bundles and sick, being herded toward the quay by several Turkish soldiers. One gray-haired old woman was stumbling along behind, so weak that she could not keep up, and a Turkish soldier was prodding her in the back with the butt of his musket. At last he struck her such a violent blow between the shoulder-blades that she fell sprawling upon her face on the stony street.

Another old woman came screaming to me, crazy with grief, crying, "My boy! My boy!" The front of her dress was covered with blood. She did not say what had happened to her boy, but the copious blood told its own story.

Mrs. Cass Arthur Reed, wife of the dean of the American College at Paradise, near Smyrna, thus describes the stripping and beating of her father, the venerable president, as also of Sergeant Crocker, an American navy officer:

"On September 11, 1922, American Marines who were on the lookout from the roof of the college notified their chief that the American settlement house, belonging to the college, was being looted by the Turkish soldiers. So the chief and father rode over to the settlement house in the college car, carrying the American flag. They informed the men that this was American property they were looting and asked why they were doing it? Father explained it was a community house and served the Turks as well as Christians in its work. They seized both men and stripped them of their clothes, valuables and money, shoes and stockings, and beat them both with a club five feet long and three inches in diameter. Sergeant Crocker was the officer who was beaten. He took the club over to the college afterward. Before he was stripped of his clothes he, of his own accord, took off his revolver and showed the Turkish soldiers that he did not mean to hurt them. They beat both men severely and separated them so they could not stand together. They beat them with the butt end of their rifles and with this big club I have mentioned. Then they demanded of Doctor MacLachlan that he hand over the Marines guarding his college. He said he was not a military man and had no control over the Marines, who had been sent by the American Government to protect the American property and the refugees in it.

"They hit him on the head, limbs, crushed the big toe of his right foot, all the time lunging at him to run, which he refused to do knowing they would put bullets in his back if he did. What he considered saved his life was that he kept calm through the whole procedure, saying they could kill him if they wished, but he wanted to explain why he was there and why he wanted them to stop robbing the Armenian property. One man lunged at him with a bayonet, and father put out his hand to grasp it and cut his palm. When the soldier drew back to get another lunge at him, the bayonet remained in father's hand. He was naked all this time. Then they lamed his left foot, breaking the tendons in the back of his knee so that he fell to the ground. He endeavored throughout the whole thing to keep his feet and he saved the blows on his head by putting up his arms. Several times they stood him up a few yards away and threatened to blaze at him."

"During this time, one of the Turkish students, who had seen the thing from the college, ran over. While the guns were pointed at father, he threw himself on the butt ends of the rifles and beseeched the men not to kill him, that he was a good man. They then accused this student of being an infidel and he swore that he was a true Moslem and he was wearing Khemal's picture on his arm and also wearing a fez. Sergeant Crocker had given the order to his men on the roof of the college not to fire or use their machine guns. Two of the Marines chased over to help when they saw what was going on. Sergeant Crocker ordered them to retreat in order to save Doctor MacLachlan's and his own life. The Turks placed Doctor MacLachlan up against a wall and were about to shoot him when, at the very moment, a young Turkish officer appeared on horseback and ordered them to desist."

Smyrna burning, with populace on quay.

They obeyed immediately and went away, proving by their immediate obedience that they were regular troops under good discipline.

The following details concerning the attack on President MacLachlan and Sergeant Crocker were furnished me by another eye-witness of the scene:

"When the bluejackets in the main building saw the predicament of their chief and that he was in danger of being ill-treated, they ran to his rescue. Sergeant Crocker spreading his arms motioned them backward, saying: 'Retire! Retire! Don't shoot! Retire!'

"This they did, and after they had covered some distance in this manner, he gave the order: 'Wheel and run!'

"They obeyed, whereupon the Turkish soldiers opened up a lively fusillade on the running Marines, and their rifle fire was so rapid and continual that it reminded me of a machine gun. Fortunately none of the Americans was hurt."

The following looting of American property occurred at Paradise, as described to me by an American lady connected with the college:

"In September, 1922, every American house at Paradise had an American flag, back and front, and all have been broken into except two.

"Lately, while the chief of the Turkish army, who had billeted himself at the president's house, was eating there with his band playing on the campus, the Turks looted the dean's house, right on the same campus."

Meanwhile, in the city of Smyrna itself, the hunting and killing of Armenian men, either by hacking or clubbing or driving out in squads into the country and shooting, caused an unimaginable panic. There was no help anywhere in sight. The battle-ships of the Great Powers, including America, could not interfere for various reasons and there were instances of persons who had reached them being sent back to the shore.

This manhunt was now being participated in by squads of the Turkish army. Armenians soon disappeared from the streets, either through death or concealment. The proclamation had been issued that any one concealing an Armenian in his house would be brought before the court-martial—a justly dreaded tribunal. One instance will show what terror this edict inspired in the hearts of all—even foreign subjects.

A prominent Dutch subject related the following incident, which he witnessed from the deck of his small private yacht:

"Over by Cordelio (a suburb of Smyrna), I saw a young couple wade out into the sea. They were a respectable, attractive pair and the man was carrying in his arms a small child. As they waded deeper and deeper into the water, till it came nearly up to their shoulders, I suddenly realized that they were going to drown themselves. I therefore pushed out to them in a boat and with the promise that I would do what I could to save them, managed to get them to shore. They explained that they were Armenians, and knowing that the man would certainly be killed and the wife, who was young and pretty, either outraged or taken into a harem and their baby left to die, they had determined to drown themselves together. I took them to several places and tried to get them in, but without success. I finally conducted them to a large school whose building and garden were full of people, rang the bell, and, when a sister came to the door explained the situation to her. When she heard that they were Armenians, she shut the door. I went away leaving them sitting on the steps of the school."

And there we shall leave them with the hope that in some miraculous way they were saved, which is not probable.

This incident is not related to throw discredit on the personnel of the foreign school. They thought that if they took in an Armenian couple, they might endanger the safety of the hundreds of people whom they were protecting, most, if not all of whom were of their own religion and therefore their especial charges.

As the Armenians had all disappeared from the streets, it was supposed that the men who had escaped had taken refuge in their own quarter, a well-built, Europeanized section of the town, within well-defined limits. Before proceeding to what happened next, it should be explained that the soldiers were helped in picking out Armenians in the streets by native spies, who accompanied them and pointed out victims. I could not recognize the nationality of those foul and slimy reptiles, the spies. I was told by some that they were Jews, but I have no proof to substantiate the statement. Of course many of the informers were Turks, and it is possible that they were all of that race, as they would naturally aid their own troops.

When Armenian hunting became too poor in the streets of Smyrna, their precinct was closed to all except Turks by soldiers stationed at the street entrances, after which the sack and massacre were conducted methodically. I did not myself attempt to enter the Armenian section, but I was repeatedly informed by those with whom I was in contact that ingress was not permitted. Americans who saw into the quarter from their windows, stated that there was not a house that escaped, so far as could be seen. All were broken into, looted, the furniture smashed and thrown into the streets. What happened to the inhabitants can easily be left to the imagination. It is easy to form a mental picture of those families, cowering in their homes, with their wives, their daughters and their babes, waiting for the crash of a rifle butt on their doors.

Chapter 17

WHERE AND WHEN THE FIRES WERE LIGHTED

IT was after this complete gutting of the Armenian portion of the town that the Turkish soldiers applied the torch to numerous houses simultaneously. As has already been mentioned, they chose a moment when a strong wind was blowing directly away from the Mohammedan settlement. They started the conflagration directly behind the Inter-collegiate Institute, one of the oldest and most thorough American schools in Turkey, in such a way that the building would be sure to fall an early prey to the flames. The pupils of that school have always been largely Armenian girls, and its buildings were, at that time, crowded with refugees. Miss Minnie Mills, its dean, a brave, competent and admirable lady, saw Turkish soldiers go into various Armenian houses with petroleum tins and in each instance after they came out, flames burst forth. In a conversation held with me on the thirtieth of January, 1925, on the occasion of the Missionary Convention that took place in the City of Washington, Miss Mills confirmed the above statements and added the following details:

"I could plainly see the Turks carrying the tins of petroleum into the houses, from which, in each instance, fire burst forth immediately afterward. There was not an Armenian in sight, the only persons visible being Turkish soldiers of the regular army in smart uniforms."

On the same occasion Mrs. King Birge, wife of an American missionary to Turkey, made the following statement:

"I went up into the tower of the American College at Paradise, and, with a pair of field-glasses, could plainly see Turkish soldiers setting fire to houses. I could see Turks lurking in the fields, shooting at Christians. When I drove down to Smyrna from Paradise to Athens, there were dead bodies all along the road."

During the same conversation Miss Mills told me of a great throng of Christians crowded into a street the head of which was guarded by Turkish soldiers. The flames were approaching and the soldiers were forcing these people to go into the houses. An American automobile passed and the poor wretches stretched out their hands, crying: "Save us! The Turks are going to burn us alive." Nothing could be done, of course, and the car passed on. Later two Catholic priests came up and said to the Turks, "This is a fiendish thing you are doing," and they allowed an old woman to come out of one of the houses.

It will be seen that the situation was such that only the Turks were in position to light the flames. Now we have the testimony of eye-wit-nesses of the highest credibility, who actually saw them commit the act. I remember on various occasions in the past talking with Miss Mills concerning Turkish atrocities, which were continually occurring and the missionary policy of remaining silent for fear of endangering the lives of colleagues working in the interior of Asia Minor. "I believe," said she, "that the time for that policy has passed and not even regard for the safety of our workers should prevent us from telling the truth." She was right, of course, for a full understanding of what has been going on in Turkey by the civilized world might have caused such a development of Christian sentiment as might have led to the taking of measures to prevent the wholesale horrors that have been perpetrated.

The following extract from a letter written by a lady connected with the American missions in Turkey has recently fallen into my hands. It is dated September 21, 1922, and was sent to a friend in the United States:

"Our Murray house across the street was locked up and protected only by an American flag hung from an upper window, but we had several Marines from the American destroyers with us who behaved splendidly all through and were a great comfort to us. Of course we had many trying things during the time we were there together, from Saturday, September ninth, until Wednesday, thirteenth, when we left, because the place was on fire. Most of the people who had fled to us for refuge behaved wonderfully patiently under the lack of bread and many difficulties. We had eighty small babies and one born there. We organized a hospital, etc., and had gotten the commissariat running with the difficulty overcome, as we supposed, of lack of bread.

"All ovens in the Christian quarters, where we were, at least, and probably everywhere, had been ordered closed from Sunday until

Wednesday, when the city burned. It looks now to me like a definite attempt to starve the population out.

"The Red Cross insisted on ovens being opened for them and the people were then burned out.

"The looting and murder went on steadily under our eyes—a murdered man lay before our Murray house door for days, under the American flag, his blood spattered over our steps, etc. There were dead and dying every where. The silence of death finally reigned over us and was broken during the last three days only by the fierce Chetas breaking in doors of houses, shooting the poor cowering inhabitants, looting, etc., and at night the howling of homeless dogs and the feet of wandering horses clanging over the rough stones of the street. After the third day of the occupation of Khemal's army, fires began to break out in the Christian quarter of the city. Miss Mills and some of our teachers saw soldiers preparing fires. I myself saw a Cheta carrying a load of firewood on his back up an alley, from which later on the fire that caught our building came.

"It is quite clear in my mind that there was a definite plan to burn out the Christian quarter after it had been looted. The time for starting the great fire was when the wind was blowing away from the Turkish quarter. I remarked when the fires began. I am sure the Turkish authorities will say one of two things, either that the retreating Greek army set the city onfire, or the Armenians. Exactly this has been published in Italian and French papers. Do not believe a word of it! We were in the Christian quarter where the fires began. Almost all Armenians except those we were sheltering had been looted and killed a day or two—even longer— before any fires began. The Greek soldiers had passed quietly through the suburbs about three or four days before.

"The whole city had been completely under military control since Saturday afternoon and the fires began on Wednesday, which finally destroyed the city. The Turks, Chetas or regulars, or both, burned the city to dispose of the dead after having carried away their loot."

The writer of this letter is neither Armenian nor Greek and is a person of the highest repute. I do not agree with the reason stated in it for the burning of Smyrna.

The torch was applied to that ill-fated city and it was all systematically burned by the soldiers of Mustapha Khemal in order to exterminate Christianity in Asia Minor and to render it impossible for the Christians to return.

By the time the Turkish soldiers had set fire to Smyrna, September 13, 1922, I had succeeded in getting hold of practically all of my colony (about three hundred in number) most of them naturalized citizens. These, together with their families and relatives were huddled in the *Theatre de Smyrne,* on the quay, owned by a naturalized American citizen. Just across the road was the harbor where the American cruiser, the *Simpson,* was moored, ready to take them off. There was a guard of bluejackets with a machine-gun inside the theater.

Soon after the conflagration took on serious proportions, I went up on the terrace of the Consulate to look. The spectacle was one of vast dark clouds of smoke, arising from a wide area, for the fire had been started simultaneously in many places.

As it was evident that the time was fast approaching when it would be necessary to evacuate the colony, I was kept very busy during those few remaining lurid hours in signing passes for such as were entitled to American protection and transportation to Piræus.

The flames consumed the Armenian quarter with such appalling rapidity as to make it certain that the Turks were augmenting them with inflammable fluids. Bluejackets sent to the scene reported that they saw Turkish soldiers throwing rags soaked in petroleum into Armenian houses.

The buildings of Smyrna were much more inflammable than they appeared at a casual glance. The city had suffered in times past from earthquakes and the stone and plaster walls contained a skeleton of wooden beams and timbers to prevent their being easily shaken down. When a wall became very hot from a contiguous fire these wooden timbers caught inside the plaster and the masonry crumbled. As the conflagration spread and swept on down toward the quay where were the beautiful and well-built offices and warehouses of the great foreign merchants and the residences of the rich Levantines, Greeks and Armenians, the people poured in a rapidly increasing flood to the water-front, old, young, women, children, sick and well. Those who were unable to walk were carried on stretchers, or on the shoulders of relatives.

The aged Doctor Arghyropolos, long a well-known figure on the streets of Smyrna, being ill, was brought down on a stretcher to the quay where he died.

The last Miltonic touch was now added to a scene of vast, unparalleled horror and human suffering. These thousands were crowded on a narrow street between the burning city and the deep waters of the bay.

The question has been frequently asked, "What efforts were made to put out the fire at Smyrna?" I did not see any such efforts. If the Turks did anything along this line it was merely the sporadic attempt of some petty officer, who had not been informed. What measures they took for saving the American consular building have already been described.

Great clouds of smoke were by this time beginning to pour down upon the Consulate. The crowd in the street before this building, as well as that upon the quay, was now so dense that the commanding naval officer told me that in ten minutes more I should not be able to get through. The hour had struck for me to evacuate my colony, to find some refuge for it in a Christian country, and to find means for its temporary sustenance.

I was profoundly stirred by the plight of these people and was determined that they should get the kindest, most generous and patient treatment possible. I therefore loaded a few trunks into a waiting automobile, as well as a few bundles of my fine collection of rugs, which fortunately were lying packed up, waiting to be taken out of their casings for winter use, grabbed whatever was dearest to me that happened to be in sight, and with my wife and a Greek servant started for the quay and the waiting destroyer.

The naval officers and men acted with the greatest efficiency and both myself and wife were treated with extreme courtesy. In the somewhat difficult task of getting us through the frantic crowds and on to the launch, the young native-born Americans were also cool-headed and capable. There was great danger of the launch being rushed and swamped by the desperate, terrified people swarming the wharf. One frightened man who jumped into it, was thrown into the sea by a young American. He was promptly fished out again and went away ashamed and very wet. It was this incident, happening at a psychological moment, and the determined guard kept by bluejackets and a few native-born Americans, which enabled us to embark and get away.

The last view of the ill-fated town by daylight was one of vast enveloping clouds rolling up to heaven, a narrow water-front covered with a great throng of people—an ever-increasing throng, with the fire behind and the sea before, and a powerful fleet of inter-allied battle-ships, among which were two American destroyers, moored a short distance from the quay and looking on.

As the destroyer moved away from the fearful scene and darkness descended, the flames, raging now over a vast area, grew brighter and brighter, presenting a scene of awful and sinister beauty. Historians and archeologists have declared that they know of but one event in the annals of the world which can equal in savagery, extent and all the elements of horror, cruelty and human suffering, the destruction of Smyrna and its Christian population by the Turks, and this was the demolition of Carthage by the Romans.

Certainly at Smyrna, nothing was lacking in the way of atrocity, lust, cruelty and all that fury of human passion which, given their full play, degrade the human race to a level lower than the vilest and cruelest of beasts. For during all this diabolical drama the Turks robbed and raped. Even the raping can be understood as an impulse of nature, irresistible perhaps, when passions are running wild among a people of low mentality and less civilization, but the repeated robbing of women and girls can be attributed neither to religious frenzy nor to animal passions. One of the keenest impressions which I brought away with me from Smyrna was a feeling of shame that I belonged to the human race.

At the destruction of Smyrna there was one feature for which Carthage presents no parallel. There was no fleet of Christian battle-ships at Carthage looking on at a situation for which their governments were responsible. There were no American cruisers at Carthage.

The Turks were glutting freely their racial and religious lust for slaughter, rape and plunder within a stone's throw of the Allied and American battle-ships because they had been systematically led to believe that they would not be interfered with. A united order from the commanders or from any two of them—one harmless shell thrown across the Turkish quarter—would have brought the Turks to their senses.

And this, the presence of those battle-ships in Smyrna harbor, in the year of our Lord 1922, impotently watching the last great scene in the tragedy of the Christians of Turkey, was the saddest and most significant feature of the whole picture.

Chapter 18

THE ARRIVAL AT ATHENS

THE destroyer reached Piræus very early in the morning, and I obtained, after some negotiations, permission from the authorities to land my colony. I was soon convinced that I had made no mistake in undertaking this task myself.

I herded my refugees temporarily in the compound of the custom-house, and immediately appointed a committee of the most capable to attend to the details of obtaining provisions, etc., and to distribute among the families the necessary sums for their daily needs from a small amount which had been provided at Smyrna for immediate necessities by the representatives of the Near East Relief. I then set about finding lodgings for my people and telegraphed to Washington an account of the situation and asked for funds. I found Piræus, as well as Athens, already crowded to saturation with refugees from Turkey. It soon became apparent that it would be next to impossible to find lodgings for these new arrivals. After running about frantically all day, toward evening I obtained permission to make use of a large steamer that was undergoing repairs in the harbor.

My appeal to Washington for financial help brought an immediate telegraphic order for two thousand dollars, and about two weeks later, Consul Oscar Heizer arrived from Constantinople with ample funds. A small room in the basement of the American Consulate at Athens was accorded to the personnel of the Smyrna office. This was crowded all day with refugees and their innumerable relatives.

It was necessary to study carefully the case of each and determine to what extent he was entitled to relief from the American Government, a matter rendered doubly difficult by the lack of essential records. The painfulness of the task was augmented by the fact that while American citizens could be repatriated, many of those dependent on them could not be sent to the United States.

Other scenes of Smyrna in flames.

The consular officials were obliged, therefore, actually to engage in the gruesome business of tearing families apart, even to the extent of separating aged parents from children, and to act as the agents of an uncompromising system which was not rising to the emergency. A more pleasant feature of the task was that of helping in the reuniting at Athens of scattered families and in obtaining news of missing relatives. This work, begun by me, was developed into an efficient system later by the Athens Red Cross.

It was very painful to me to be thrown into daily contact with the beggared inhabitants of Asia Minor, whom I had known such a short time before as self-supporting and prosperous. I remember with peculiar distinctness the old guide of my hunting expeditions, an industrious small farmer from the village of Develikeuy. Many an unforgettable day have I spent in the pinewoods with him, shooting woodcock and hare and swapping Greek and American hunting yarns in his native tongue. The day before I left Athens, I met him wandering about the streets in a dazed condition. He told me that his beautiful and intelligent young daughter, who was soon to have been married, had disappeared; he feared that she had suffered a fate worse than death.

Mr. Heizer, on taking over the work, asked me the peculiar feature of the job. I knew he was a very competent man, as he had done most of the work of the Constantinople Consulate for years, so I replied, "The quality most needed in this task is a human heart and not to try too much to repress its promptings."

From his reply I understood that he was aware of this requisite and agreed with me. I therefore left my people with him without apprehension and sailed to the United States on leave granted me by the department!

Chapter 19

ADDED DETAILS LEARNED AFTER
THE TRAGEDY

AT Athens, at Paris, and later in the United States, I met various eye-witnesses of the great disaster who related to me things that they had seen. I have made notes of the testimony of several of these persons, carefully excluding all such as were Greek or Armenian, not with the feeling that statements made by such would necessarily be unreliable, but rather that it might be impugned as prejudiced.

American relief workers, standing on the deck of a ship, which left Smyrna soon after the *Simpson,* related that they saw a man throw himself into the sea and swim toward the vessel. A Turkish soldier raised his rifle, took aim and blew the man's head off. Another American, in relating the same incident to me, added the detail that the Turk pointed his rifle over the shoulder of a British Marine. Teachers and others of the American Girls' school told me that they saw a lady who resided in the house directly across the street standing in the road surrounded by Turkish soldiers, who were robbing her and tearing the rings from her fingers. When they finished, one of them stepped back and cut one of her hands off with his sword. The lady was never seen again and doubtless died as the result of her injuries.

The story has frequently been told by Americans and others who were at Smyrna that a crowd of residents, men, women and children, had gathered on a lighter lying in the harbor but a short distance from the pier, with the hope that some Entente or American launch would tow them to a ship and save them. The Turks threw petroleum on them and burned them all to death. A confirmation of this dreadful story was furnished me by Miss Emily McCallam, directress of the Intercollegiate Institute of Smyrna. She arrived in that ill-fated city on the morning of September 14, 1922, after the fire set by the Turks had been raging all night, and saw a number of charred bodies floating in the harbor, which she was informed were the corpses of the people cremated on the lighter.

A prominent Dutch merchant of Smyrna, who had taken refuge on his yacht during the fire, related to me at Athens that all through the night of the dreadful thirteenth he heard fearful screams from the shore, ending suddenly in a queer watery gurgle. He learned the next morning that a lot of throats had been cut.

A book of great human interest could be written by any one who cared to interview the refugees and set down the stories he would thus hear of hair-breadth escapes and the desperate and ingenious expedients resorted to. One wealthy woman with a large family of small children saved them all in the crush and panic by tying a long rope around their waists, the other end of which she attached to her own. A lady living at Vourla, a large town near Smyrna, saved her beautiful daughter by skillfully disguising her as a bent and ugly crone. A woman in the United States, an American citizen, wrote me that her baby girl, four years old, whom she had left in Smyrna with grandparents, had turned up in one of the islands. During the massacre this little tot had crept into an open grave where she lay as still as a mouse for many hours, until she heard people speaking English, when she made herself known and was rescued by friendly hands.

There are horrible tales told of the burning of the sick in the hospitals and of children in the schools. The pupils in the American schools and institutions were practically all saved, as also the orphans entrusted to our care.

Just before I left the city, the Greek high-commissioner turned over to me a considerable sum of money belonging to an orphan asylum which he had founded at Boudja, a suburb of Smyrna, and asked me to take charge of the institution and the children in it. I did so and organized an American committee to carry on the work. The children were all saved and got away to Saloniki, owing largely to the heroism of Mr. Murman, a young American. There is no doubt, however, that many Greek children, attendants of the schools in the center of the burned area, perished in the flames, and that numerous sick lost their lives in the same way. What the number was can not be determined, but in view of the rapidity of the spread of the fire, any safe evacuation of the hospitals was evidently impossible.

Wholesale violation of women and girls was one of the outstanding features of the Smyrna horror. It is necessary to mention this disgusting subject, though not to dwell upon it; it can not be possible that the Christian people of America for material advantages will be in sympathy with a policy of coddling a race that specializes in such conduct. On this point a letter is submitted by Doctor M. C. Elliott, a noted and native-born American physician who for several years was engaged in hospital work in the Near East. Doctor Elliott's testimony that she has never yet seen a Mussulman woman who had been violated is significant and, incidentally, is high tribute to the Greek soldier. It will be seen, also, that Turks confine their lustful orgies to Christian girls. Here is Doctor Elliott's letter:

AMERICAN WOMEN'S HOSPITALS

NEAR EAST BRANCH

GREEK UNIT

Athens, Greece   June 2, 1923.

Consul-General George Horton, American Legation, Athens, Greece,

My dear Mr. Horton:

How true Gladstone's famous statement was in regard to the Turk's character has been most amply proved in the late Smyrna disaster.

My position as a woman physician makes me peculiarly well placed to know about the treatment of young girls by the Turks. In my four-year experience in Turkey I think it is a rather remarkable fact that I have yet to see the Turkish girl or woman who has been ravished. As a marked contrast to this I have seen hundreds of Christian girls who have been in the hands of Turkish men. The late Smyrna disaster was no exception to this and I can justly come to the conclusion from what I have seen with my own eyes that the ravishing of Christian girls by Turks in Smyrna was wholesale. I have actually examined dozens of such girls and have had the story from them of the experiences of other girls with them. By actual examination I have proven that their story in regard to this was not exaggeration, so I have no reason to believe the statement they made in regard to their companions was not true.

The treatment of girls in Smyrna during the late disaster of 1922 is unspeakable and I am willing to go on record as an American physician and as director of an organization doing a very large medical work in Greece following the Smyrna disaster, as having made this statement.

Sincerely,

(Signed) DOCTOR M. C. ELLIOTT,

Director American Women's Hospitals, Athens, Greece.

Among other witnesses of the Smyrna outrage was an employee of the great firm of MacAndrews and Forbes, of New York. Their offices at Smyrna were in the fire-devastated area. This man saw Turks throwing hand-grenades into buildings, which later caught fire.

A prominent Y.M.C.A. official, a native-born American, related to me the following:

"I was standing with several others on the deck of a ship, watching the fire, when I saw some persons throwing some liquid against one of the large buildings directly on the sea, and very soon the building burst into bright flames. Turkish soldiers were patrolling up and down in front of the building at the time and did not interfere."

A well-known Y.M.C.A. worker informed me at Athens that he saw women stabbed with bayonets by Turks and the bodies of children who had been thus stabbed. His progress through the town in an automobile while on errands of mercy, was impeded by corpses.

While I was in Washington during 1922 and 1923, I saw much of Doctor Esther Lovejoy, the well-known woman physician of New York. Doctor Lovejoy had arrived in Smyrna while the refugees were still on the quay and the evacuation was going on. She literally threw herself into the work of giving medical aid to the sick and wounded, and especially to women in childbirth. She described vividly to me the robbing of the refugees by Turks, soldiers and civilians—both on the water-front and at the moment of their embarking. While our men were helping these unfortunate people to get away, the Turks were pawing them over, women and men, searching through their clothes for any money or valuables that they might have on them.

One of the most outrageous features of the Smyrna horror was the carrying away of the men between the ages of eighteen and forty-five. These were inoffensive farmers and others, in nowise responsible for the landing of the Hellenic army in Asia Minor. They were the breadwinners and their forcible detention left the widows and orphans to be supported by the so-called "Christian nations," especially the United States. It requires but little imagination to picture the scene as it was described to me by Doctor Lovejoy and others, who told of children throwing their arms about the legs of their fathers and shrieking for mercy, and of wives clinging to husbands in a last despairing embrace; and it takes less imagination to visualize the manner in which these couples were torn asunder.

This last scene on the Smyrna quay reveals the whole diabolical and methodically carried-out plan of the Turks. The soldiers were allowed to glut their lust for blood and plunder and rape by falling first on the Armenians, butchering and burning them and making free with their women and girls. But the Greeks, for whom a deeper hatred existed, were reserved for a slower and more leisurely death. The few that have been coming back tell terrible tales. Some were shot down or killed off in squads. All were starved and thousands died of disease, fatigue and exposure. Authentic reports of American relief workers tell of small bands far inland that started out thousands strong.

The Turks allege that they carried off the male population of Smyrna and its hinterland to rebuild the villages destroyed by the Greek army on its retreat. This has a ring of justice and will appeal to any American unacquainted with the actual circumstances. The Greek peasants of Asia Minor were Ottoman subjects, in nowise responsible for the acts of the Hellenic government. Very few enlisted voluntarily in its armies and they used every influence and subterfuge imaginable to avoid fighting. Had the Greeks of Asia Minor been a stout warlike race and had they cooperated strongly with the Greeks of the mainland they could have kept the Turks at bay.

The object of Khemal, as we have seen, was one of simple extermination. The reason alleged was one of those shrewd subterfuges used by the Turks to fool Europeans. But not all the unfortunates carried away by the Turks were Greek men. Many thousands of Christian women and girls still remain in their hands to satisfy their lusts or to work as slaves. A report submitted to the

League of Nations gives the number as "upward of fifty thousand," but this seems a very conservative estimate. The United States should sign no treaty with Turkey until these people are given up.

Mustapha Khemal made a stupendous blunder when he burned Smyrna and maltreated its inhabitants. Had he used them kindly, irrespective of religion, they would all have rallied loyally around him and he would have shown himself a really great man. Moreover, such a move would have been a splendid triumph for Mohammedanism.

Chapter 20

HISTORIC IMPORTANCE OF THE DESTRUCTION OF SMYRNA

THE destruction of Smyrna by the Turks was an event of great significance in Church history. At the time of the birth of the Prophet, about A.D. 570, Christianity had covered, in addition to the area known in general to-day as "Europe," the ancient province of Asia, extending as far east as the Caspian Sea, a broad strip of Syria, and a wide belt of North Africa clear across to the Atlantic Ocean.

In A.D. 30, according to Kurtz, historian of the Christian Church, there were five hundred Christians in the world; they had increased to five hundred thousand by A.D. 100, and they numbered thirty million in the year 311.

Asia Minor and Africa are famous in the history of the Church as the habitat of many of the most famous Christian fathers and martyrs, such as Polycarp of Smyrna, Tertullian of Carthage, Clement of Alexandria, Chrysostom of Antioch, Origen of Tyre, Cyprian of Carthage and a host of others. Saint Paul was born in Tarsus of Cilicia.

In the eighth century, Timotheus sent a band of missionaries from Mesopotamia to convert the Tartars, who went as far as the Caspian Sea, and even penetrated into China, "planting and reviving in those parts a knowledge of the gospel." The Seven Churches of Revelation were in Asia Minor, and the fact that Smyrna was the last of these, and kept her light burning until 1922, emphasizes the significance, in Church history, of her destruction by the Turks.

The object of the Emperor Constantine in founding his capital was to build a distinctly Christian city that should be the metropolis of Christendom. Its splendors, its refinement, its art and culture, its wealth, its power, its fame as a center of learning and of piety are unforgettable even to-day. In the presence of its gentlemen and great dames, the knights and ladies of Western Europe were mere boors and hoydens. Wrecked, plundered and mis-managed by the Latin knights, a calamity from which it never recovered, there was enough of its culture left, when the Turks finally laid hands on it, to scatter over Europe and regenerate the West. The Renaissance, that wonderful awakening from the darkness of the Middle Ages, was largely due to the learning brought into Europe by the scholars of Constantinople, fleeing from the Turk. Those scholars had kept the light of the old classic culture burning during all the years of European darkness and ignorance.

If Constantinople could have been spared and Christianity saved in the Near East, the results to civilization would have been incalculable. What a glorious city a Greek Constantinople would be to-day, if it had always stayed Greek, with its long traditions and its immense treasures of ancient culture! Another and more beautiful Paris, bestriding the Bosphorus, great in commerce, learning, science and all the graces and influences of Christian civilization.

Thus says Sir Edwin Pears, in his well-known history:

"The New Rome of Constantine Augustus passed under the power of a horde of Oriental adventurers, Turanians by original descent, mongrels by polygamy. This was the greatest victory ever won by Asia in her debate with Europe. For many decades thereafter there seemed at least a possibility that the East might destroy all the fruit of Marathon."

Quoting again from the same author:

"Under the rule of its new masters Constantinople was destined to become the most degraded capital in Europe, and became incapable of contributing anything whatever of value to the history of the human race. No art, no literature, no handicraft even, nothing that the world would gladly keep, has come since 1453 from the Queen City. Its capture, so far as human eyes can see, has been for the world a misfortune almost without any compensatory advantage. Poverty as the consequence of mis-government is the most conspicuous result of the conquest affecting the subjects of the Empire. Lands were allowed to go out of cultivation. Industries were lost. Mines were forgotten. Trade and commerce almost ceased to exist. Population decreased. The wealthiest state in Europe became the poorest; the most civilized the most barbarous. The demoralization of the conquered people and of their churches was not less disastrous than the injury to their material interests. The Christians lost heart. Their physical courage lessened."

This description of the condition of Asia Minor as the result of the capture of Constantinople continued down to the ultimate complete destruction of the Christians by the Turks. Nothing changed in the nearly five centuries that have passed. The Turk has not altered either in his character or his methods. The scenes described by Pears as following the taking of the Queen City, the massacres and violation of women, were duplicated at Smyrna, with the added horror of the sufferings of the Christians on the quay.

After Constantinople, Smyrna, "Ghiaour Smyrna," became the last stronghold of Christianity and Greek culture in the Near East. It had its great and valuable libraries, its learned men, its famous schools. The Greeks and Armenians could at any time have attained safety by abjuring their faith. Yet, though there have been apostates, they have, in general, kept the faith and have suffered.

The only civilization that has existed in Turkey since that black year, 1453, has been that supplied to it by the Christian remnant of the old Byzantine Empire. For that reason the work of the American and other missionaries took on a great importance. They went out originally to Turkey to convert Moslems. They found that they could not do this, but that their real mission was with the Christians, who were eager to be uplifted and enlightened. The recent rapid development of the latter in advanced agriculture, industries, commerce, education, was restoring Christianity in the Orient and reknitting the wasted and torn fabric of the old Byzantine Empire. To the great Christian Powers was given a tardy and last opportunity of repairing the wrong that was done the world when St. Sophia, the Temple of the Eternal Wisdom, fell into the hand of the Turk.

Chapter 21

NUMBER DONE TO DEATH

HOW many were massacred in Smyrna and its dependent towns and villages? It is impossible to make any estimate at all accurate, but the efforts to minimize the number must at first glance fail of credence.

Official statistics give the Armenian inhabitants of Smyrna as twenty-five thousand and it is certain that the larger part of the men of this community were killed, besides many women and girls, also numerous Greeks. A dispatch to the *London Daily Chronicle* of September 18, 1922, says: "The lowest estimate of lives lost given by the refugees, places the total at one hundred and twenty thousand."

Reuter's Agency, in a dispatch of the same date, makes the following statement: "From none of the accounts is it possible to give the exact figures of the victims, but it is feared that in any case they will be over one hundred thousand."

Mr. Roy Treloar, newspaper correspondent, wired as follows: [*] "Nureddin Pasha commenced a systematic hunting down of Armenians, who were gathered in batches of one hundred, taken to the *Konak* and murdered."

The *London Times* correspondent telegraphed: "The killing was carried out systematically. Turkish regulars and irregulars are described as rounding up likely wealthy people in the streets and, after stripping them, killing them in batches. Many Christians who had taken refuge in the churches were burned to death in the buildings which had been set on fire."

Mr. Otis Swift, correspondent of the *Chicago Tribune,* visited the Greek islands on which refugees had been dumped by the rescue steamers and saw many of the victims of the tragedy, whose stories and the nature of whose wounds bore additional testimony to the ferocity of the Turks. Here is a short quotation from Mr. Swift's report: "Hospitals of the Greek islands are crowded by people who had been beaten and attacked by the Turks. In a hospital at Chios I saw a child who still lived, although shot through the face by a soldier who had killed its father and

---

[*] September 20, 1922.

violated its mother. In the same hospital there was a family of six orphan Armenians. A four-year-old baby of this family had been beaten with rifle butts because no money had been found sewn in its clothes."

There is no doubt that many thousands of the defenseless inhabitants of Smyrna and the surrounding country were done to death by Turks.

To the number actually killed on the days of the massacre must be added the deported Greeks who perished, the people who died in the flames or were killed by falling walls, those who expired on the quay and those who have since succumbed from want, injuries or grief. The extent of the catastrophe can be realized from the magnitude of the relief work that has been carried on ever since, and from the immense sums which have been raised, principally in America, for the maintenance of the widows and orphans.

The following statement is from Mr. Charles V. Vickery, Secretary of the Near East Relief, 151 Fifth Avenue, New York:

"In regard to the amount of money which has been spent on relief, I would say that so far as the Near East Relief is concerned the total of money and supplies contributed by the American people has amounted to approximately ninety-five million dollars. So far as I know there are no available statistics of the amounts spent by other countries. The largest contributor has of course been Great Britain, but we do not have any figures here in our office.

"In answer to your second inquiry as to how much is still necessary, would say that it is extremely difficult to make an answer that would be reliable as there are so many uncertain factors in the problem, as you know only too well. So far as the Near East Relief is concerned, our program should very rapidly diminish after another year or two and the Executive Committee has definitely adopted a resolution to the effect that there shall be some sort of coordination or amalgamation of Near East agencies at the end of five years or sooner if practicable. This resolution was adopted approximately nine months ago.

"Near East Relief will need around four million dollars a year for the next two years if present indications are reliable."

One of the most important reports connected with the fire is that of the Reverend Charles Dobson, British chaplain of Smyrna, and a

Smyrna at the Height of the Fire.

committee of prominent Englishmen, all inhabitants of the district, including the British chaplains of Bournabat and Boudja. This report throws the responsibility of the fire upon the Turks, "whose fanatic elements, fed by the license of three-days' looting, fired the city in the hope of driving out the non-Moslem and non-Jewish elements." Such a report from such a source, leaves no doubt as to the fact that Smyrna was burned by Turks, although these gentlemen do not take into account the circumstance that the town was in complete control of Khemalist troops at the time and that regular soldiers of the Turkish army, in uniform, were seen by abundant witnesses to set the fires. It is pertinent in this connection in that it relates incidents of greater ferocity than I have yet given, but which I refrain from quoting.[*]

---

[*] The entire report can be found in the *Gibraltar Diocesan Gazette,* No. 2, vol 6, November, 1922.

Chapter 22

EFFICIENCY OF OUR NAVY
IN SAVING LIVES

THE following radio messages were received by me on the evening of September thirteenth, while at sea, en route to Athens, and after:

Litchfield
Simpson   9-13-22.
0113 fire has almost reached Consulate. Consulate has escaped with practically all official matter of value. A large number of other Americans have been taken on board and now being taken on board but have no complete muster as yet. Entire population on water front have placed many orphans and employees of American benevolent associations on *Winona* with request but not order to evacuate them to Athens promising your assistance in matter of their landing, 2220 Litchfield Capt.

Simpson   9-14-22
For Horton. *Winona* leaving 4 P.M. to-day for Piræus with three hundred and fifty refugees directed to report to you for instructions about evacuation. Simpson awaits arrival *Winona* due about 9 A.M. Friday signed Hepburn—1130 Capt. (file)

Simpson rdo   9-15-22
                                                             0800
    Direct for Horton. 0114 ref my 0114 dash 1136 *Winona* will have about 1000 refugees destroyer *Odsafl* left 7 A.M. for Salonica with 600 all she could carry. Please announce and assist evacuation if possible.. Hepburn 1900—

Simpson rdo   9-15-22
S. S. *Winona*   7.00 A.M. date
                                                             848
Consul-General Horton, *U.S.S. Simpson*—Winona arrives 11 A. M. to-day with refugees. Please arrange to expedite debarkation. Short of provisions—Walter Master.

Simpson rdo   9-15-22
                        Litchfield   Time 1850
Simpson   0848
1014 for Horton Am Consul September 14th, 5 P.M.
Consulate completely destroyed by fire last night. Code funds
and valuable documents saved. Three-fifths of city now
burning and no apparent possibility of stopping fire. Your
personal property including car lost. Credit Lyonnais in midst
of fire zone and manager and staff gone. Signed, Barnes.

Chapter 23

RESPONSIBILITY OF THE WESTERN WORLD

CONCERNING the manner in which the Turk has always profited from the conflicting interests and jealousies of Christian powers, Lord Morley made the following shrewd remark years ago:

"This peculiar strife between Ottoman and Christian gradually became a struggle among the Christian Powers of Northern and Western Europe to turn tormenting questions in the East to the advantage of private ambitions of their own."

This comment of the famous Englishman was voiced before the full dawn of the Petroleum Age, and while as yet America's chief interest in Turkey was the protection of a few missionaries.

A brief review of the political situation, which afforded the Turks unbridled license to "raise the hand of violence," is here necessary. It will be evident that they have again profited by their well-known policy of exploiting the dissensions and conflicting interest of Christian powers. They have been as sensitive as a barometer to the least sign of dissension among European governments or peoples, and have shown extraordinary shrewdness in provoking or augmenting it.

The Turk was the ally of the Germans during the Great War, and perhaps his most useful one. Practically all the gold disappeared from Turkey and there is only one place to which it could have gone. The Turkish Empire was ransacked for wheat and other food supplies. Long train-loads of foodstuffs, marked "Berlin" were moved with great frequency toward Constantinople from Smyrna and other distant points. He held the Straits stoutly against the British and French, and one of his proudest and most frequent boasts to-day is that he defeated them there. Germany, one of the great-civilized powers, was the ally of the Turks while they were carrying on the extermination of the Armenians. After the defeat of Germany, it was taken for granted that the bad days of the Christians of the Ottoman Empire were over. Turkey was paralyzed.

Mustapha Khemal, who burned Smyrna and completed the destruction of the Christians, is a creature of Europe. It can not be denied that the original plan of the Allies included the partition of the Ottoman Empire and that various projects were formed and promises made which could not be realized on account of conflicting interests, and that the Turks were aided by one or the other of the Powers either secretly or openly to defeat the ambitions of rivals.

In the course of this sad history, Christians were armed against their hereditary oppressors and then left to the vengeance of the latter. In general, they were abandoned, as no Christian power desired to offend the Turk, from whom great benefits were expected, to be in turn showered on the subjects of the power that showed itself most Turkophile. The United States did not abstain from this gruesome competition. In the beginning, interest prompted the spread of what came to be a well-nigh universal pro-Turk propaganda in Christian countries. When the fearful death harvest of this sinister sowing began to be reaped, fear of popular indignation and disapproval gave rise to a policy of suppression of the truth and to anti-Christian propaganda.

During my days in Saloniki, 1910–14, both Italy and Austria were supposed to be looking forward to an early occupation of that city and their battle-ships made frequent visits there, vying with one another in the lavishness of their hospitality to the inhabitants. The common subject of conversation was, "Which will have Saloniki, Austria or Italy?"

Chapter 24

ITALY'S DESIGNS ON SMYRNA

AUSTRIA'S imperial designs were extinguished by the outcome of the Great War. Italy's, however, burned more brightly than ever. In an article in *Foreign Affairs* of June 15, 1923, Mr. Francesco Coppola says:

"Although Italy entered the war to combat the German attempt at hegemony and to wrest her historic frontiers and the control of the Adriatic from Austria, Italy's traditional instinct really aimed to secure the indispensable modicum of security and freedom for expansion. It was for this reason that in the fundamental pact of alliance—the Treaty of London of April, 1915—Baron Sonnino stipulated for Italian colonial compensation in Africa in the event of a Franco-English partition of the German colonies, and for a corresponding zone in Southern Anatolia in the event of Allied acquisitions in the Levant. It was also for this reason that, later on, when he got wind of the complete plan of a tri-partite division of the Ottoman Empire, (disloyally concluded in 1916 between France, Russia, and England without the knowledge of Italy, who had been fighting for more than a year by their side), he forced the Allies to reopen the question and to give an adequate share to Italy. The new treaty was discussed in April, 1917, between Sonnino, Ribot and Lloyd George at St. Jean de Maurienne— from which it took its name—and was concluded and signed in London in August of the same year. While leaving Constantinople and the Caucasus, Armenia and part of the Anatolian coast of the Black Sea to Russia, Syria and Cilicia to France, and Mesopotamia and the protectorate over Arabia to England, this treaty assigned to Italy Southwestern Anatolia, the whole vilayet of Aidin with Smyrna, the whole vilayet of Konia with Adalia and a small part of the vilayet of Adana. But this very treaty contained the poison which was later to weaken it. Even before the war was over, the Allies hastened to avail themselves of the pretext of the absence of Russia's signature to denounce the Treaty of St. Jean de Maurienne. Thus it came about that in the spring of 1919, Lloyd George, taking advantage of the weakness and temporary absence of

Orlando, and violating the treaty of St. Jean de Maurienne and the armistice of Mudros, was able to arrange that Smyrna and the surrounding neighborhood be given to Greece. This was done with the full consent of Wilson, who, absolutely ignorant of European and Mediterranean affairs, blindly allowed himself to be governed by idealistic impulses and natural prejudices and with the approbation of Clemenceau, who was only too delighted to be able to *jouer un mauvais tour a l' Italie.'"*

Some of the Italian publicist's conclusions are open to discussion, but his article sets forth the Italian frame of mind. There was much talk at Smyrna during the time of the Greek occupation in military circles and among the Levantines about Italian efforts to build a port farther to the south, in the vicinity of ancient Ephesus, that would become the chief harbor of Asia Minor and leave Smyrna to sink into insignificance. Many stories were told also of Italian efforts to win the affections of the Turk. In any case, it is certain that bands of Turkish marauders were in the habit of crossing the line from the Italian zone and of attacking and killing Greeks, after which they would take refuge with the Italians, where they could not be pursued.

The statement that the Turks received munitions and many arms from Italian shippers was persistently repeated, and has never been successfully refuted. The Italian viewpoint has already been explained. They considered that Smyrna had been promised them and that the Hellenic forces had been hurried there by their unfaithful allies to forestall their own landing. Italy can consider herself very fortunate that she did not beat the Greeks to Smyrna, for even with her own resources, so superior to those of King Constantine, she would have had her hands full.

But, the point is, her attitude contributed to the Greek defeat, the burning of Smyrna and the final destruction of the Christians of Asia Minor. Much valuable Italian property was destroyed as well as that of others. An aftermath of Italian antipathy to Greece may be seen in the bombardment of Corfu and the seizure of the island by the Italian fleet on August 31, 1923.

On the twenty-seventh of the same month, five Italian members of the commission for the delimitation of the frontier between Albania and Greece were waylaid on a lonely road in Albania and foully murdered by unknown persons. The demands of the Italian Government, including a payment of fifty million liras, were refused by the Greeks, on the ground that culpability had not been established. A request by Greece that the affair be referred to the League of Nations was refused and the island bombarded, with the result that sixty-five civilians, largely refugees, were killed or wounded. The indignation of the Italians is easily understandable, but a knowledge of preceding events is necessary to explain the wholly unnecessary bombardment of a Greek island on insufficient data and the killing or the wounding of sixty-five entirely innocent persons. As these latter were killed by cannon, they were not, of course, murdered.

Chapter 25

FRANCE AND THE KHEMALISTS

FRANCE'S participation in the Near Eastern tragedy is well known. Her motives are not far to seek: A frank, bitter and undiluted hatred of King Constantine and everything connected with him, and suspicion of England's expansion in a region to which France herself has been devoting great attention for many years. French capitalists and the French Government have been investing heavily in Turkey and Gallic propaganda has been pushed by a vast network of Catholic schools officially supported, whose object, in so far as the government's interest is concerned, has been to catch the natives young and make Frenchmen of them. British or other expansion and predominating influence in Turkey has meant the imperiling of the great sums invested and the annulment of years of patient labor.

This invasion of the Ottoman Empire is admirably set forth in a lecture delivered in 1922 by Monsieur Passereau, Director of the French Commercial Bureau of Constantinople, and published *in extenso* in the *Echo de France* of Smyrna. Extracts are herewith given:

"To-day one unconsciously associates such places as Constantinople, Jerusalem, Beirut, Syria and the Lebanon with French influence, and here are in fact presented almost innumerable proofs of the many ways in which the French now exert and have for a long time exercised a vast and beneficial influence from one end of the Orient to the other.

"Our schools, our welfare institutions, hospitals, asylums for the aged, homes for the foundlings and orphanages are established in every port in the Levant. In every city of the interior, in all of the important villages, along the entire length of the railways completed or under construction, there are French instructors, people who teach the children our name, our language and our history.

"Let us now make a survey of French financial interests in the Ottoman Empire and see to what extent French influence has made itself felt in this connection. Some of these interests are herewith listed and enlarged upon:

"Ottoman Public Debt: France's share of the Public Debt, external and internal, is 250,000,000,000 francs, or 60.31% of the capital of the entire debt. The remainder of the debt is principally divided between England and Germany, the former holding 14.19% and the latter 21.31%;

"Turkish Loans: The history of governmental loans in Turkey dates back to the Crimean War. Since that time, France has without cessation, upon every occasion where the public debt was threatened by internal difficulty, intervened either in the form of assistance in reorganization or financial subscription;

"French Private Enterprises in Turkey: France has approximately 1,100,000,000 francs invested in private concerns in the Ottoman Empire. Her participation in the industrial activities of the Empire aggregates 53.5% of the total, as opposed to 13.68% enjoyed by Great Britain and 32.77% by Germany. These organizations embracing activities in the form of banks, railways, ports, electric power plants, telephones, tramways, etc., extend over the entire domain of Turkey and surround the economic life of the Orient with a network of French interests. (Among interests of this sort mentioned by the lecturer are the Imperial Ottoman and other banks, the tobacco monopoly, etc.)

"Railways: France has under construction and exploitation 2,077 kilometres, with an invested capital of 550,238,000 francs, as opposed to Germany's 2,565 kilometres and England's 610. France has 42,210,000 francs invested in mines in Turkey, besides about 80,000,000 in quays and ports."

In addition, the lecturer gives a list of thirty-nine important miscellaneous enterprises, including industrial, commercial, insurance, shipping and other corporations. It should be remembered that the investments listed above were made in gold.

French sentiments, especially as regards England, are revealed in a work by the French writer, Michel Paillares, entitled *Le Khemalism devant Les Allies,* published in 1922. Monsieur Paillares is one of the editors of the journal *L'Eclaire* of Paris.

The following quotation is from one of the conversations held by Paillares with French officers at Constantinople, showing their strong pro-Turk, anti-Christian and anti-English feelings:

"I am introduced to an officer in command. He is a man all of one piece. He does not mince his words. He is like a man carved out of rock, for he is unmovable in his sympathies and his antipathies. Like the lieutenant of the Navy whom we have already heard, but more furiously still, he is the enemy of the Armenians, the Greeks, the Jews and—the English."

"'As for me,' he snaps, 'there is not even room for discussion! We ought to be completely, absolutely Turkophiles—I will say more, Turkoenthusiasts (Turcomanes). I love the Mussulmans and I hate their non-Mussulman subjects, who are rubbish. Assure these brave men their independence and their territorial integrity and we shall have in them the most faithful and the most loyal of allies. What do we seek here! A rampart against Russia and British imperialism! The maintenance of our prestige! The free development of our commerce, the expansion of our language! The respect of our schools and colleges! The safeguarding of our financial interests! We shall have all that by means of a French-Turkish collaboration. We ought no longer to hear the Jeremiads of the Armenians and the Greeks and the Jews. We must no longer play the game, neither of England nor of Russia. Russia, although split up by Bolshevism, must always be watched. She has intentions with regard to this country, which we must not encourage. But I do not think that she is an immediate danger. It is Great Britain, which, above all, is becoming troublesome. We are, nearly all of us (French officers) for the Khemalists and against the British and the Greeks."

Though this is the opinion of a single individual, it expresses pretty clearly the general French attitude of mind as shown by French policy since the Armistice. It is evident that the sentiments of this French officer and of his colleagues, for whom he speaks, display a keen note of discord among the Allies, helpful to the Turk even in his gruesome work of massacring Christians.

Professor Davis says in A Short History of the Near East:[*]

"In August, 1922, apparently with French munitions and French counselors, the Khemalists suddenly attacked the Greek positions in Bithynia. The Greeks were in poor morale, worn out by long campaigning and miserably led. Their army was utterly routed and evacuated Anatolia with almost incredible speed. The Turks drove straight onward to Smyrna, which they took (September 9, 1922)

* Page 393.

and then burned. The world was again horrified by one of the now standardized Ottoman massacres of conquered populations."

It is to be noted that neither the French nor the Italians permitted the Greek navy to search the ships of their nationals proceeding to Turkish ports, which is in itself a breach of neutrality and can have but one interpretation—that they were carrying arms and supplies to the Khemalists, with the consent and protection of their governments.

For these reasons the battle-ships of the brave and chivalric French, "Protectors of the Christians in the Orient," were obliged to sit quietly among the dead bodies floating in the Bay of Smyrna and watch the massacre going on.

The following typical incident illustrates the perfect harmony prevailing in naval circles in the Harbor of Smyrna resulting from international discords and how punctiliously the amenities were observed: An admiral of a battle-ship had been invited to dine with one of his colleagues. He arrived some minutes late and apologized for the delay, which had been caused by the dead body of a woman getting tangled up in the propeller of his launch.

That lucid and well-informed writer, Doctor Herbert Adams Gibbons, in an article in the *Century Magazine* for October, 1921, gives the best analysis of the French and Italian attitude with regard to the Turks that I have seen anywhere. It can not, of course, be reproduced *in extenso* here, but a few quotations will be sufficient to show that French support of the Turks was due to fear and jealousy of the British. Says Doctor Gibbons:

"The British regarded Greece as a sort of protectorate, financially and militarily under the control of Great Britain. The scheme was spoiled by the fall of Venizelos and the subsequent defeat of the Greek armies in Asia Minor."

"The Near East had been culturally French since the Crusades. From Saloniki to Beirut, France was determined to reign supreme. Palestine represented the very last concession that it was possible for the French to make. Of course the French did not hope to possess Constantinople, but they were not going to let the British settle themselves on the Bosphorus, as they had done at Gibraltar and Port Said, in Malta and Cyprus. For this would mean British domination of the Mediterranean and the Black Seas, and for British capital and

British goods the priority in markets which had been traditionally French."

"I am not conjecturing. The trend of the French press, inspired by the government, leaves no room for doubt as to what is prompting France to send arms and money to Khemal Pasha."

"During the war one of the telling indictments against Germany was her friendship for and alliance with Turkey when the Armenians were being massacred. Germany was held responsible for the massacres on the ground that she could have stopped them had she used her influence with her ally. This was true; but is it not equally true now that France must bear the opprobrium and in a measure the responsibility, of the Armenian and Greek massacres of 1920 and 1921? A French general negotiated with the Nationalists in Cilicia without stipulating that the massacres should cease. French diplomats have negotiated with the Angora Government of Khemal Pasha, conniving at the massacres of Armenians and Greeks. The sole thought of the Germans during the war was to use the Turks and not run any risk of offending them by protesting against the massacres. This is exactly what the French are doing now."

This is plain talk and—horrible. The question that naturally arises in the mind of any decent American is, what, if anything, was the United States, the great Christian country, the hope of the world and fountain of missionary activities, doing while all this was going on? What influence was she using, what resounding note of protest and horror was she giving utterance to?

Various historical events connected with the French pro-Turk, but really anti-English activities, are interesting to the student of diplomatic psychology, and the ease with which peoples can be influenced in their predilections and hatreds by those governing them.

At a critical period of the War, on the Balkan front, the Allies demanded the demobilization of the Greek army, the surrender of half of the Greek fleet and a great part of the Greek artillery. King Constantine, after his successful campaigns in the Balkans, had become an object of almost divine worship to the Greeks, and the Allies were afraid of him. On December 2, 1916, a party of French Marines marched into Athens to take possession of the Greek material demanded. They were fired on by Greek soldiers and a number of French Marines were killed.

This was a most regrettable act on the part of the Greeks, and foolish. It was more foolish to send a few foreign Marines into a capital city to drag off its artillery and expect them to be received with open arms. This unfortunate event is the basis to-day of deep-seated hatred of French against Greek.

G. F. Abbott, in his work, *Greece and the Allies,* gives the results of the so-called "Battle of Athens" as follows:

"And so the 'pacific demonstration' was over, having cost the Greeks four officers and twenty-six men killed and for officers and fifty-one men wounded. The Allied casualties were sixty killed, including six officers, and one hundred and seventy-six wounded"

On April 10, 1920, the Khemalists treacherously massacred the French garrison at Urfa, killing one hundred and ninety men and wounding about one hundred more, and on October 20, 1921, Franklin Bouillon, in the name of the French Republic signed a separate treaty with the Turks. Immediately after the burning of Smyrna he rushed to the still-smoking city and, seizing Mustapha Khemal in his arms, kissed him.

This kiss of Franklin Bouillon has become historic, and while bearing no resemblance to a certain other famous and sinister caress, deserves to rank with it as one of the two most famous kisses in sacred and profane history.

Chapter 26

MASSACRE OF THE FRENCH GARRISON IN UFRA

THE facts of the massacre of the French garrison at Urfa, obtained from original sources, took place under the following conditions:

The Nationalists had been besieging the small French force in Urfa during the early days of April, 1920, and at length Commander Hauger was compelled to capitulate. On the eighth of April he decided to evacuate the city and did so under the following terms: That all Christians should have ample protection; That the houses occupied by the garrison should not be reoccupied by the Turks until the garrison had left the city; that the graves of the fallen should be respected; that sufficient transport should be supplied to convey their arms, ammunition, etc.* One officer of the gendarme and ten men would accompany them for safe convoy.

These were agreed to by the Mutessarif of Urfa and the commander of the Turkish Nationalist forces, but, notwithstanding this arrangement the French were attacked shortly after they had left the town and nearly annihilated.

A native-born American who chanced to be in Urfa on relief work and who desired to proceed to Aleppo decided to accompany the ill-fated expedition and was an eye-witness of what happened. The following account may be interesting as a chapter of authentic history, never before published:

"We left Urfa at one-thirty a.m. on Sunday the eleventh of April, 1920, Captain Perraut being with the advance guard, four gendarmes leading the way, in center of column the officer of gendarmerie, Emir Effendi, who was to accompany us to our destination.

"On passing the crest of the hill we observed several gendarmes and we were informed that this was their post. The ascent was very difficult as, the horses were in bad condition owing to lack of food

---

* Their own transport being sadly depleted.

Portion of the three hundred thousand persons who fled to the water-front in the destruction of Smyrna. They were a human wall two miles long, the blazing city behind and the Aegean Sea before them.

and exercise. The camels delayed us as they were well-laden and climbed very slowly. We halted as usual ten minutes to the hour, the rear guard consisting of one hundred and fifty to one hundred and sixty men, being two kilometers in the rear.

"At six a.m., passing through a ravine on to a straight stretch of road, we were suddenly attacked from the rear and both flanks, the enemy having machine guns among them. The firing commenced before the camels had passed out of the ravine. They were in the bend and halted. Previous to the attack, I had been marching with Commander Hanger and five minutes before the firing commenced was riding on a Red Cross wagon containing two wounded. When the firing commenced, two wagons which preceded the others, having their horses and mules wounded or killed, were forced to halt. I jumped down, taking cover in a hollow at the roadside, and finding that I was exposed to fire from the hilltops, decided to make my way forward trusting to find the Commander, who I knew was only two yards in advance.

"By this time the attack had taken a formidable form. The ground here formed a basin surrounded by hills and bare of any cover so that the column was forced to go forward to find a position of defence, which they did five hundred yards ahead. The transport with the above exception, was thus cut off, most of the horses by that time being killed. Firing by this time had become extremely heavy, and going forward I joined Commander Hauger and two other officers in a hole in the hillside, which had been left by some stonecutters and from where he directed operations. We were afterward joined by two other officers and the Turkish officer of gendarmerie, who was then disarmed, and two interpreters."

"About nine a.m., the rear guard were heard and the firing became very heavy. We were shortly joined by the officer who had been in charge of them, who gave us a thrilling account of what had happened; they had been ambushed in a gully, very few escaping.

"From a hill to the north, we observed the Turkish Nationalist flag. Shortly after this, several Kurds were seen coming over the hills, apparently a tribe. At ten o'clock or thereabouts, Commander Hauger held a conference and decided to surrender.

"At this time the line was broken to the east, the transport was lost and the rear guard cut up and many wounded were coming in. He then told the officer of the gendarmerie to go out with a flag of truce.

"As we had several Armenians with us who needed protection, I suggested that I might accompany him. To this he agreed, and taking my interpreter carrying the American flag, myself carrying the white flag with the gendarme in the center, we proceeded toward the enemy's position. We were fired on continually. On reaching the destroyed transport column, we came upon a large body of troops and asked for their commander. We were informed that they were without one, being irregular troops, 'Chetas, etc.'

"I then instructed the officer of the gendarmerie to send off messengers to stop the fire and this was accomplished about ten twenty a.m. A few minutes afterward a mob of Kurds rushed from the hills toward the French positions, and the battle recommenced. Seeing that it was impossible to do anything *as they refused the truce,* I told the officer of gendarmerie to ride to Urfa, a distance of about nine miles, to inform the Mutessarif of what had happened and to bring carriages for the wounded and this he did.

"Here I witnessed the killing of wounded and the killing of men, *who were surrendering their arms.* To this, there are many witnesses, including Lieutenant Deloir, who at present is a prisoner in Urfa. I demanded a guard of gendarmes who had by this time arrived to accompany me to Urfa. We proceeded, encircling a hill and striking the road at a natural cistern where we were able to get water. The officer commanding the gendarmes of Urfa arrived and gave me a further guard of six men, instructing them to get to the city as soon as possible, the tribesmen showing great hostility. We proceeded by a circuitous route through a ravine, arriving in Urfa about two thirty p.m., having walked for twelve hours, and bringing with me a Syrian, Jacob, who had been working at the Swiss mission at Urfa.

"I was unable to save any Armenians as they were not to be seen.

"Note: The prisoners, some fifty, are in hospital and perhaps another fifty are in prison. There may be more, but at present it is impossible to say as there is a possible chance that some may still be with the Kurds. The official report of the Mutessarif says that they buried one hundred and ninety, and one hundred in hospital and prison brings the number to roughly three hundred, whereas the garrison when en route numbered more than four hundred.

"Sundry notes: Lieutenant Deloir, before mentioned, was stripped by Turkish regular cavalry and rescued in a nude condition by Kurds who found him some time afterward and who fed him and brought him to Urfa.

"The Syrian Yakub, whom I brought back with me and who was trying to escape to Aleppo is now in Urfa. The Armenians have not been heard of.

"When crossing the battle-field, I observed a company of Turkish infantry regulars and the machine section with mule transport proceeding toward the French positions. They were, perhaps, a little late unless there had been action in the hilltops and were going forward to continue to fight.

"The attack took place in the hills west of Urfa about nine miles from town and two miles from junction of Arab Punar, and Seroudj roads."

The above story is given precisely as received by me, without alteration, even of punctuation. The characteristic features of this incident are:

The breaking of the agreement; the use of so-called "irregulars" by the Turkish authorities to escape responsibility and the presence of regulars in case of need; the killing of the wounded and of those giving up their arms.

There were present in Urfa during the siege Mrs. Richard Mansfield, widow of the famous actor; Mr. G. Woodward, accountant of the Near East Relief; and Mary Caroline Holmes, a heroic American lady who wrote a book on her experiences, entitled *Between the Lines in Asia Minor,* published by the Fleming H. Revell Company.

The part played by Italy and France, which so greatly contributed to the extermination of the Christian population of Turkey, and the fearful events at Smyrna, are well summed up by George Abbott in the work above referred to, in the following words:

"France, who since the Armistice had displayed a keen jealousy of England's place in a part of the world in which she claims special rights, presently concluded a separate agreement with Turkey—an example in which she was followed by Italy—and gave the Turks her moral and material support against the Greeks; while England, while refusing to reverse her policy in favor of their enemies, contented herself with giving the Greeks only a Platonic encouragement, which they were unwise enough to take for more than it was worth."

Chapter 27

THE BRITISH CONTRIBUTION

UNFORTUNATELY, I am restrained from writing many interesting facts connected with a history of this kind; some of the things that came to my knowledge in my official capacity. To the honor of Great Britain, however, I believe that there were moments when she came within a hair's breadth of living up to her best traditions. What prevented her at the critical moment, I have never learned.

At any rate, the British contribution to the Smyrna horror did not consist in active aid of the Turks, neither did she furnish them with arms or munitions. But, though she was largely responsible for the landing of the Greeks in Asia Minor, and the latter were defending her interests, she afforded them no aid, but gave them fallacious encouragement, which led them to their doom. As far as England was concerned, Greece was the victim of British internal politics, which seized upon the government's policy in the Near East as an object for attack. If Lloyd George was pro-Greek, his political opponents became—*ipso facto*—rabid pro-Turk. If the Hellenic soldiers were mere tools of the British, as both the Italians and French believed, then it certainly was not "playing the game" to desert them in their extremity; and this desertion carries a graver responsibility with it, inasmuch as it made possible the fearful catastrophe of Smyrna and its hinterland.

Chapter 28

TURKISH INTERPRETATION
OF AMERICA'S ATTITUDE

OF our American responsibility for the destruction of the Christians of
the Near East, I write with great hesitation and sorrow and must confine
myself to the statement of certain universally known facts.

The days and months leading up to the fearful events at Smyrna
were noisy with the Chester concession and pro-Turk propaganda. The
enthusiastic pro-Turk articles in the press of the two Chesters—father
and son—are still fresh in the public memory. Other pro-Turk and anti-
Christian writers were busy, some among them doubtless earning their
daily bread. The Turks were in funds. They had been busy picking the
bones of the Christians and had laid their hands on great sums.

The shrewd Europeanized group of Turks, who inhabit
Constantinople, overdid themselves in the courtesies and hospitality,
which they lavished on foreign diplomats. This sort of Oriental is the
most plausible and fascinating man in the world. The educated hanum,
also, is extremely charming, and has a seductive grace that is hardly
granted to her alien sisters. If a few of them take off their veils and show
their lovely faces in Constantinople, they have little difficulty in
persuading diplomats that they are emancipated and that polygamy is a
thing of the past among Mohammedans; that the Greeks burned
Smyrna, that a million and a half Christians practically committed
suicide and were not actually massacred, or anything else they wish.

What can one do but believe when he is taken back to the days of
Haroun al Raschid, and floats off to a palace perfumed with roses of
Cashmere on an enchanted carpet?

Our representative at Constantinople, Admiral Mark L. Bristol, is an
extremely attractive personality: honest, brave, generous, with frank and
winning manners. By the sheer magnetism of his genial and engaging
character he gathers about himself, wherever he is, a school of admirers
and disciples who ardently defend the admiral and everything that he
thinks and does.

The naval officers who came to Smyrna at the Consulate's request
were typical of the American naval officer in general, high-type

intelligent gentlemen, of an efficiency that may be described as well-nigh perfect. They were under certain orders at Smyrna, which it was incumbent upon them to carry out. They accomplished all their duties there thoroughly and correctly and performed prodigies after the fire in saving refugees.

I was somewhat puzzled, however, when an American lady at Smyrna informed me that one of the officers had told her that he was "pro-Turk." Another, a commander, made the same remark at Athens, at luncheon, during one of the trips, which the destroyers were making back and forth between that city and Smyrna.

While stopping at the Army and Navy Club in Washington in 1922, I asked a naval officer of high rank if it was true that he was pro-Turk, and he replied:

"Yes, I am, because I was brought up as a boy to the belief that the Turks were always chasing Greeks and Armenians around with a knife. Well, I have been over there to Constantinople several times and I have never seen anything of the kind, so I have come to the conclusion that it is all buncombe."

This is all right. Every man is entitled to his opinions, no matter on what evidence or process of reasoning founded. My surprise was due to the fact that I had thought that the officers who came to Smyrna were under orders to be neutral.

I was sitting in the wardroom of one of our destroyers moored in the harbor of Smyrna. At a moment when the massacre had begun to assume alarming proportions, a newspaper correspondent, a passenger on the same naval unit, entered the room, opened his typewriter and began to write. When he had finished about half a page, he read it carefully, took it out of the machine, and said:

"I can't send this stuff. It'll queer me at Constantinople. I must get busy on Greek atrocities." I have often wondered what he meant. I was sitting quite close to him and heard him very distinctly.

Let us briefly review the situation which enabled the Turks in the year of our Lord, 1922, to complete the extinction of Christianity in the Near East: The Germans were, as long as they lasted, the active allies of the Turks, and during this period nearly a million Armenians and many thousands of Greeks perished; after the Armistice and during the period which led up to the destruction of Smyrna and the accompanying massacre, the French and Italians were allies of the

Turk, and furnished him moral and material support; the British gave no aid to the Greeks, but contented themselves with publishing an account of the dreadful events that had been taking place in the Ottoman Empire; the Americans gained the reputation of being pro-Turk, true friends, who would ultimately, on account of this friendship, be given the permission to put through great schemes, which would result in the development of the Ottoman Empire and, incidentally, fill certain American pocketbooks. The Turks confidently believed that commercial avarice would prevent us from interfering with their savagery, or even strongly condemning it.

Never in the world had the Turk so good an opportunity to glut his lust for Christian blood without fear of interference or criticism.

The first Lausanne Conference closed, after reaching no agreement, on February 7, 1923, and the second opened on April twenty-third of the same year. On April tenth, still of the same year, the National Assembly at Angora ratified the Chester Concession. As the terms of this concession conflicted sharply with British and French interests, the date of its ratification is highly suggestive.

This concession is dead now, and there was never enough in it to cause a serious row between the United States and any European power. The State Department has denied the official support of this scheme and must be believed. This, however, has not prevented a general conviction in Turkey that it was a project under the especial protection of the American Government. Such a belief is very easy to create in Turkey, where even the Mission Schools are popularly supposed to be government institutions.

At any rate, it is not probable that great sums of American capital will flow into Turkey under present conditions. Whatever public sentiment may be, or whatever apathy may exist as to the fate of some millions of our fellow creatures, who howl annoyingly when they are massacred or if their families are torn apart, or if they are robbed of homes, capital is cautious; it does not believe in railroads built in a country of ruined cities, nor does it connect massacre with prosperity and progress.

And in all this tangle of conflicting interests, during which the Turk continued massacring, the thoughtful observer is impressed with one thing— the clearness of John Bull's vision and the directness and tenacity of his purpose; he knew what he wanted and he took it. There are copious oil wells at Maidan i Naftun, from which the oil is piped down to Mukamra, not far from Basra, on the Persian Gulf, where the British landed early in the war. There are rich oil fields at Mousul. General Townsend was on his way there when the Turks stopped him at Kut el Amara, but that did not stop Cousin John. He is at Mosul now and the Turks would have liked to give Mousul to Admiral Chester and the others. No wonder the State Department says that it kept out of that.

Chapter 29

THE MAKING OF MUSTAPHA KHEMAL

THE building up of Mustapha Khemal by certain Christian countries was one of the unwisest, most pernicious and most dangerous deeds that Occidental diplomacy, intrigue and jealousy has ever perpetrated. It is a legend among Mohammedan peoples that the Turk is the "Sword of Allah," "the Defender of Islam," and "the Scourge of the Unbeliever." As he is the lowest of Mohammedans intellectually, with none, or at best few, of the graces and accomplishments of civilization, with no cultural history, the other disciples of the Prophet do not consider him as their intellectual or moral equal.

In only one particular has he always kept abreast of the age, and that is in the art of war. He is perhaps the only example of a great and scientifically warlike nation that is great in nothing else. He destroys but can not construct. Even the other Mohammedans, who have been subjected to his rude and blighting sway, have continually fought to be freed from it, and have only joined him in common cause against the Christians.

Of him, the historian Butler says:

"The Goth might ravage Italy, but the Goth came forth purified from the flame, which he himself had kindled. The Saxon swept Britain, but the music of his Celtic heart softened his rough nature. Visigoth and Frank, Heruli and Vandal, blotted out their ferocity in the very light of the civilization they had striven to extinguish. Even the wildest Tartar from the Scythian waste was touched and softened in his wicker encampments, but the Turk, wherever his scimitar reached—degraded, defiled and defamed, blasting with eternal decay Roman, Latin civilization, until when all had gone he sat down satisfied with savagery to doze into hopeless decrepitude."

But Mohammedans do not forget that it was the Turk who took the great and splendid city of Constantinople, the last bulwark of Europe against the devastating and enslaving hordes of Asia; that it was the Turk who firmly established himself in Europe on the field of Cossova; that it was the Turk who destroyed the flower of the Hungarian chivalry—twenty thousand together with their king—on the stricken field of Mohacz in 1526, and three years later arrived at the gates of Vienna, which he besieged; that a little over a hundred years later a Turkish horde again stormed the Austrian capital, which only the timely arrival of a Polish army saved.

At the close of the Great War the Turk was beaten to his feet and his prestige ruined. "The Sword of Islam" had been broken. The victory over the Greeks, though with the aid of European officers and material, and the spectacular destruction of Smyrna with the massacre of its inhabitants, revived the legend of the conquering and avenging Turk. "The Sword of Islam" had been welded again, to conquer and destroy. The noise of that event resounded and is still echoing throughout the Moslem World, in Egypt, in India, in Northern Africa and in Syria.

And more than that, the rise of Mustapha Khemal, creature of divided Christendom, of the mutually jealous and internecine Occident, has given new courage to all the yellow and black and brown peoples, whom Kipling describes as "the White Man's Burden," who while they may cut one another's throats over the question of Mohammed or Confucius or Buddha, are united in their hatred of the white man.

The ferment in the East is the bubbling up of a deeper feeling, than the careless or unobservant thinker wots of: It is the revelation of a profound and fundamental antipathy. The East is tired of being civilized by superior peoples; of being educated and converted; of being shoved off the side-walks; of being called "Eurasians" and having their daughters ostracized if they marry whites; of having their children excluded from white schools; of being discriminated against in immigration laws.

One can not say that the West is entirely wrong in attempting to maintain its prestige and its Occidental civilization, but he can safely affirm that the hatred that has been steadily growing in the Orient is deep and implacable, and that the result will be murders, uprisings, little wars, big wars. The maker of this statement may be set down as an alarmist. So is the man who sticks up the sign at the railway crossing, "Stop! Look! Listen!" The dissension in the Western World that made it possible for the Turks to make a clean sweep of Christian civilization in the Ottoman Empire, to burn Smyrna and massacre its inhabitants in sight of a powerful fleet of European and American war vessels, has added unknown weight to the "White Man's Burden."

That a mutual hatred of the West is bringing together peoples hitherto antagonistic and of different creeds is confirmed by Lothrop Stoddard in his book, *The New World of Islam,* quoting the writer, H. Vambery, the authority on Moslem affairs:

"The change in Moslem sentiment can be gauged by the numerous appeals made by the Indian Mohammedans at this time to Hindus, as may be seen from the following sample, entitled significantly, 'The Message of the East':

"'Spirit of the East,' reads this noteworthy document, 'arise and repel the swelling flood of Western aggression! Children of Hindustan aid, aid us with your wisdom, culture and wealth; lend us your power, the birthright and heritage of the Hindu! Let the Spirit Powers hidden in the Himalayan mountain peaks arise! Let prayers to the God of Battles float upward; prayers that right may triumph over might; and call to your myriad gods to annihilate the armies of the foe!'"

Let the reader compare this appeal of Mohammedan to Hindu with the spirit of the article from the *Progres de Salonique* of July 22, 1910, quoted in an early chapter of this book, in which Turkish Mohammedans and Japanese Buddhists, etc., are conceived as having common cause against Western civilization. That Oriental peoples believe that their opportunity will come from the dissensions and wars of Western nations, which they are watching with much interest and satisfaction, was expressed as early as 1907 by Yahya Siddyk, an Egyptian judge and writer of Mohammedan faith, who seems to have foreseen the Great War:

"Behold these Powers ruining themselves in terrifying armaments; measuring each other's strength with defiant glances; menacing each other; contracting alliances which continually break and presage those terrible shocks which overturn the world and cover it with ruins, fire and blood!"

Chapter 30

OUR MISSIONARY INSTITUTIONS IN TURKEY

SOME of our missionary schools and colleges in the Ottoman Empire are open for business, and reports of the Mission Board describe them as flourishing. They are either continuing or resuming operations after having suffered their share of pillage and massacre. The Board of Missions is making an earnest and vigorous campaign for raising more American money to be sent into Turkey for their upkeep.

As a church member, as an ex-official who has been of service to those institutions on many occasions, I am obliged to state that I have serious doubts as to the wisdom of contributing further money to our religious establishments in the Ottoman Empire under present conditions. Before doing so the fact should be widely advertised in Turkey that their real object and that of the men and women working in them, is, by hook or crook, to convert the Turks to Christianity, which is considered to be a religion superior to Mohammedanism. American church people should be informed frankly that the prohibition of the teaching of Christianity or the holding of Christian religious exercises has been accepted by the Mission Board; and that no effort to convert Turks is countenanced by the Ottoman Government. But this is really no new thing, as Christian proselytizing in Turkey has never been possible; the understanding that religious teaching is to be confined by the missionaries to the members of their own families and to teachers already of the Christian faith, is recent.

Soon after the entrance of the Khemalists into Smyrna a committee of Moslems visited one of our schools and expressed the most friendly sentiments to the teachers:

"We hope you will keep right on with your good work and we promise you every support, only you understand that there is to be no more religious teaching."

When I mentioned this to Mr. Jacobs, of the Y.M.C.A., he replied: "Where L— is and C—" mentioning two missionaries, "Christ will be taught somehow." But, if that is so, the Turks ought to know it. Any other course is not quite honest nor up to the standard of the old time Christians who testified in heathen lands and suffered martyrdom. Moreover, the Mohammedan's contempt of the Christians is very easy to arouse and it would be a sad thing should it enter the mind of the Turks that some of the missionaries were willing to forego the teaching of their faith to save their buildings and their jobs. Even though this is not true, it would not be difficult to create this impression.

It seems hardly probable that the Mission Board would come out and officially inform the contributing church members of the United States:

> "We have no intention or desire, either immediate or ultimate, of converting Mussulmans in Turkey. We are running secular schools there with the hope of raising their general moral standing and making Mohammedans of them."

If the board can raise money for such a purpose, that would be a frank honest proposition for both Turk and Christian.

It is logical for the devout Christian to give money for the conversion of the Moslem. The faith of the Nazarene is one of the proselytizing religions, as Professor Max Muller said in his famous lecture in Westminster Abbey in 1873. It can not be possible, however, that there is any mental impulse in this country which would lead Americans to contribute large sums for the support of purely secular schools in foreign countries. Even from a humanitarian standpoint, there are more crying needs for their charity.

The one thing that the missionary working in Turkey really fears is that some Turk may be converted. Should this occur a storm of fanaticism and violence would break upon his head that might close his school and end his career. It is not possible to convert Mohammedans in Turkey, nor even let them get wind that one is trying to do such a thing. In my thirty years of service in the Near East I have known of but one Moslem really converted. I remember distinctly the uneasiness, which his impending public confession caused among his teachers, imperiling, as it did, all their future activities. He was persuaded by the missionaries that the time was not

MISS MINNIE MILLS
Teacher in American Girls' College at Smyrna, who saw Turkish
soldiers engaged in firing Armenian houses.

ripe for him to proclaim his change of faith, but the Mohammedans became aware of it and promptly murdered him. According to the best information available it cost between forty-five and eighty million dollars to convert that unfortunate young man and he did not last long.

The Moslem who renounces his religion suffers ostracism, forfeiture of his goods and practically commits suicide. During the War and before the Turks severed diplomatic relations with the United States, the Germans were anxious to seize the beautiful and expensive buildings of the International College of Smyrna and turn them into barracks. I had much to do in preventing this. On one occasion, while talking with Rahmi Bey, the Turkish governor (*vali*) of Smyrna at that time, he said to me: "The only reason that I can protect that college is that I have never seen any disposition on the part of its president and faculty to convert Moslems. Should any such attempt be made I could no longer shield it." This was the argument, which the *vali* used with the authorities at Constantinople. It was this clean record which saved the college.

The missionaries in Turkey now find themselves in the position of hostages. They have seen many of their buildings destroyed, their native teachers, Armenians and Greeks butchered, their pupils scattered. They have received no help from the American Government. They are in the hands of the Turks. Many of them have spent their lives in the work and not a few of them own comfortable modern homes, which they have paid for in part or entirely.

That very shrewd and capable Scot, Doctor Alexander MacLachlan, has built up the International College at Smyrna by a lifetime of earnest and persistent effort. Its beautiful and expensive buildings, erected with money raised in America, his own substantial home, the delightful residences of the faculty, situated in charming gardens, are all resting on a powder mine. An outburst of fanaticism might sweep this idyllic picture from the face of the earth at a moment's notice; might make it one with the desolate ruins of Smyrna but a few minutes' distant. It would need but a tiny spark to set off the powder mine—some adverse criticism of the Turk, the conversion of a Mohammedan. The danger for this, as well as for similar institutions, is augmented by the fact that the ignorant, fanatical population of the Ottoman Empire is greatly in the majority, and there is abundant evidence that the Spirit of the Prophet is abroad, impatient of reform.

One missionary, at least, has been in the United States loudly proclaiming Mustapha Khemal the George Washington of Turkey, and comparing the soldiers who burned and sacked Smyrna and violated its women with the veterans of Valley Forge. This has doubtless got back to Asia Minor and has produced a salutary effect. One word more: Our missionaries have been operating in Turkey for nearly a century. They did admirable work among the native Christians, but what evidence have the Turks shown in their conduct of any results obtained from the vast sums sent into their country for their enlightenment and moral uplifting? It is impossible to argue with a religious devotee of any creed. The question is put to the normal men and women of America.

Chapter 31

AMERICAN INSTITUTIONS
UNDER TURKISH RULE

THIS cursory account of the methodical extermination of Christianity at the hands of the Turk should convince any one that he now has no intention of allowing it to be revived and propagated in his domains in foreign schools. An earlier chapter gave an account of the aid and support, both moral and financial, furnished American missionary and philanthropic institutions by the Greeks during their occupation of the Smyrna region, and at Saloniki. The following statement of their treatment under Turkish rule is from the pen of Dana K. Getchell, well known in missionary circles:

"In 1914, when the World War began, Anatolia College, Marsovan, Turkey, had an enrollment of four hundred twenty-five students and the Girls' School had about three hundred; a total of about one thousand individuals all together were on the American premises, including professors' families, servants and their families and the American colony. At the close of 1914, the Americans had just finished the building of a large hospital which was occupied by the Turks before the American doctor had the opportunity of moving in.

"In 1915, the Armenian deportation took place in the early spring of that year. Out of our faculty of fifteen native teachers and a servant list of fifteen more, twenty of these individuals, men, were deported and, as far as the college authorities knew, were killed, as they have never been heard from since.

"Our college steward, during this time, went to the market for his usual work and never returned. A noted Turkish lawyer of the city, at that time connected with the college, informed me that if I would go with him to a certain spot in a vineyard near the city he would show me the well into which this man's body was thrown. He was perfectly in sympathy with this deed that was committed.

"During the month of June, 1915, I escorted a party of ten American ladies and children to Constantinople, via Angora, the Black Sea route having been closed. While in Constantinople, I learned of the deportation of the Armenians in the interior, especially from Marsovan and vicinity. I worked for days to get permission from Talaat Pasha to return to Marsovan, but his excuse was that 'things were doing' in the interior and it was not a good time for foreigners to be traveling. Later, upon hearing that more than four hundred Armenians had crowded into the American premises, information was taken to Talaat and his promise received that no Armenian within the American premises should be deported. Upon the strength of this promise, I sent a telegram to my associates in Marsovan, and having received permission to travel in those days, I hastened back to my work. Upon my arrival in Marsovan, I found that the first great deportation of those sheltered in the American premises had taken place the day before.

"Two days later, the Turkish gendarmes and police came to our premises and demanded the girls, forty-nine in number, from the American school. These demands were persisted in and on that day, by the order of the Turkish Government, all these girls were started on the road to Sivas, a journey of six days interior from Marsovan. Two of the American teachers, Miss Willard and Miss Gage, by persistence, secured permission to follow these girls one day after they had started on their journey and overtook them just as they were entering Sivas, six days later. By working with the *vali* of the province for days, permission was finally given to these American ladies for all these girls to return to the Girls' School at Marsovan.

"At the beginning of the deportations in 1915, Marsovan was inhabited by twelve thousand Armenians. When the deportations were finished scarcely one thousand of that nationality could be found in the city. This complete destruction of the Armenians in this city is only an example of what took place throughout the Vilayet of Sivas.

"In January, 1916, the Greek deportations from the Black Sea began. These Greeks came through the city of Marsovan by thousands, walking for the most part the three days' journey through the snow and mud and slush of the winter weather. Thousands fell by the wayside from exhaustion and others came into the city of Marsovan in groups of fifty, one hundred and five hundred, always under escort of Turkish gendarmes. Next morning these poor refugees were started on the road and destruction by this treatment was even more radical than a straight massacre such as the Armenians suffered before.

"In 1917, in the dead of winter, a second deportation of Armenians from the Black Sea coast began and the same treatment was undergone by those who were obliged to flee from their homes.

"On May 16, the fifteen Americans, men, women and children were obliged to undergo this hardship—to leave their homes and property—for this long overland journey. On that date the American premises were occupied by Turkish soldiers and the buildings all taken over as a base hospital.

"Six weeks later four of this group returned to Marsovan by permission from Talaat Pasha, with the understanding that they would be able to occupy their homes and use the school buildings for educational purposes. The buildings, with the exception of the houses, which were obtained with great difficulty, were never returned but were in constant use by the Turkish military authorities up to the time of the Armistice, March, 1919.

"The treatment of Americans and American property throughout Turkey was the same as that experienced by the Americans in Marsovan. The schools and colleges in Sivas, Cæsarea, Harput, Aintab and other places were closed and for the most part the American workers were sent out of the country. Since the Armistice, this same treatment of Americans throughout the interior has continued. The schools have not been allowed to open and property to the value of many thousands of dollars, has continually been occupied by Turks."

In December of 1914, Turkish soldiers seized the American mission property of Afion Kara Hissar and occupied the church, school and pastor's house for a period of four years, leaving the buildings with doors, windows and roofs wrecked and generally defiled with human offal. The Turks pulled the Cross down from the church and put the Crescent up in its place. In 1919, the Turks seized these buildings again and housed soldiers in them.

The proposition under which our Christian schools may now operate in Turkey is about as follows: Will you please let us repair our buildings at our own expense with money raised in America, and reopen them in those places where enough human beings remain to furnish a few pupils, and educate Turkish boys in English, arithmetic, etc., if we give our solemn word that we will not teach them any Christianity?

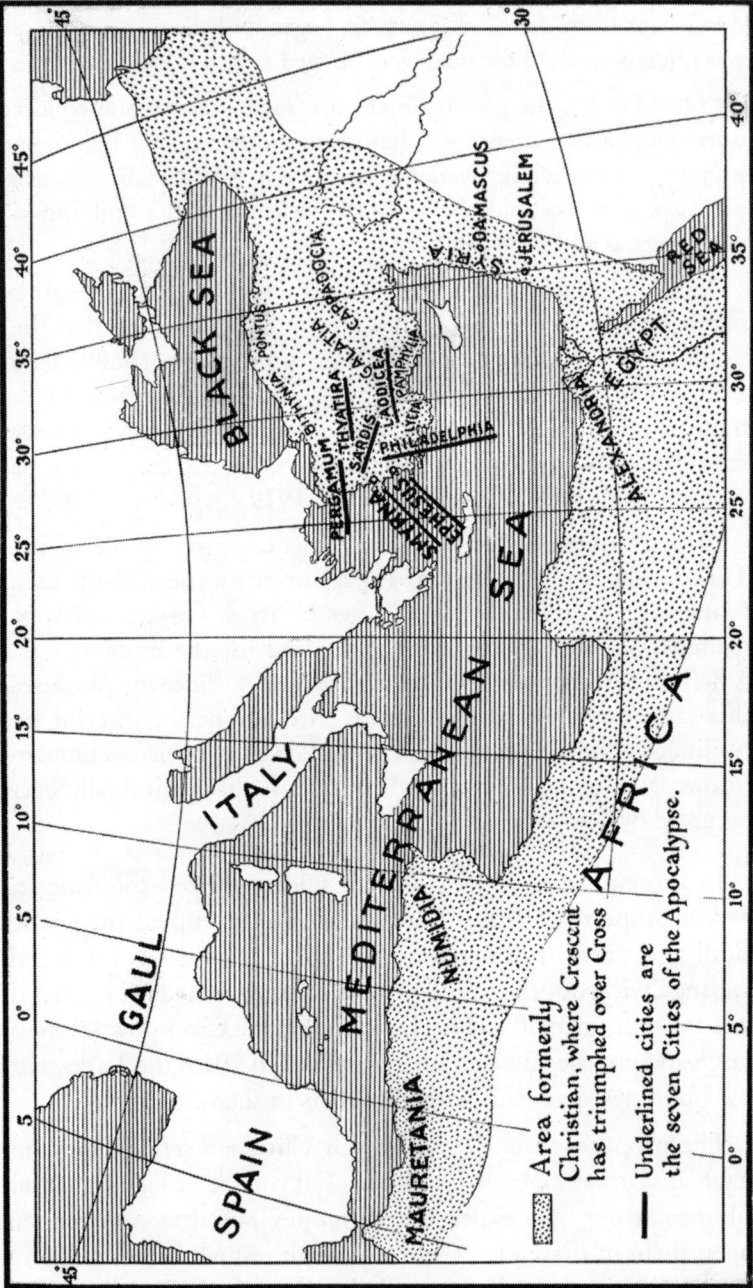

Area formerly Christian, where Crescent has triumphed over Cross

Underlined cities are the seven Cities of the Apocalypse.

SPAIN

GAUL

ITALY

MAURETANIA

NUMIDIA

AFRICA

MEDITERRANEAN SEA

BLACK SEA

PONTUS

BITHYNIA

GALATIA

CAPPADOCIA

PERGAMUM

THYATIRA

SARDIS

PHILADELPHIA

LAODICEA

PHILADELPHIA

EPHESUS

SYRIA

DAMASCUS

JERUSALEM

ALEXANDRIA

EGYPT

RED SEA

Much consolation is derived in certain quarters from the fact that no religious education of any kind is permitted in Turkish schools, and it is argued that the measure is not aimed particularly at Christian institutions. People who obtain comfort from this feature of the case are evidently not aware that the Turk is familiar with all the different ways of skinning a cat. They do not give him credit for the peculiar brand of intelligence which he certainly possesses. At any rate, the result is the same, in so far as the continuation of foreign evangelical work in Turkey is concerned.

The above is a very moderate and unprejudiced account of what has been done, in part, to the American educational institutions in Turkey, but gives no idea of the actual ferocity shown to students and teachers and the material damage wrought.

I was talking recently to a prominent clergyman, friend of the one-time president of one of the greatest missionary colleges in Turkey, who made the following statement:

"Some time ago, I was talking with the President of one of the American Colleges in Turkey who told me of the frightful treatment of the people in the town where he was located. He told me the college was closed and the professors, their wives and families driven out and some sixty or seventy of them were put to death. The tears streamed down his cheeks as he said: 'I can see those dear, good people at this moment, as they were marched away by the heartless Turk.'"

Regarding the conditions under which the American missions are now operating in Turkey, Samuel M. Zwemmer says, (1924):

"Recent regulations regarding foreigners in Turkey and the prohibition of Christian teaching to Moslem children in Mission schools do not indicate a larger degree of liberty under Islamic Nationalist Government, but rather a recrudescence of the old spirit."

If the reverend gentleman had said, "A continuance of the steadfast and unalterable policy", he would have been nearer the truth.

Doctor James L. Barton, Secretary of the American Board of Commissioners for Foreign Missions, of Boston, Massachusetts, has an interesting article in the *Homiletic Review* of January, 1924, on

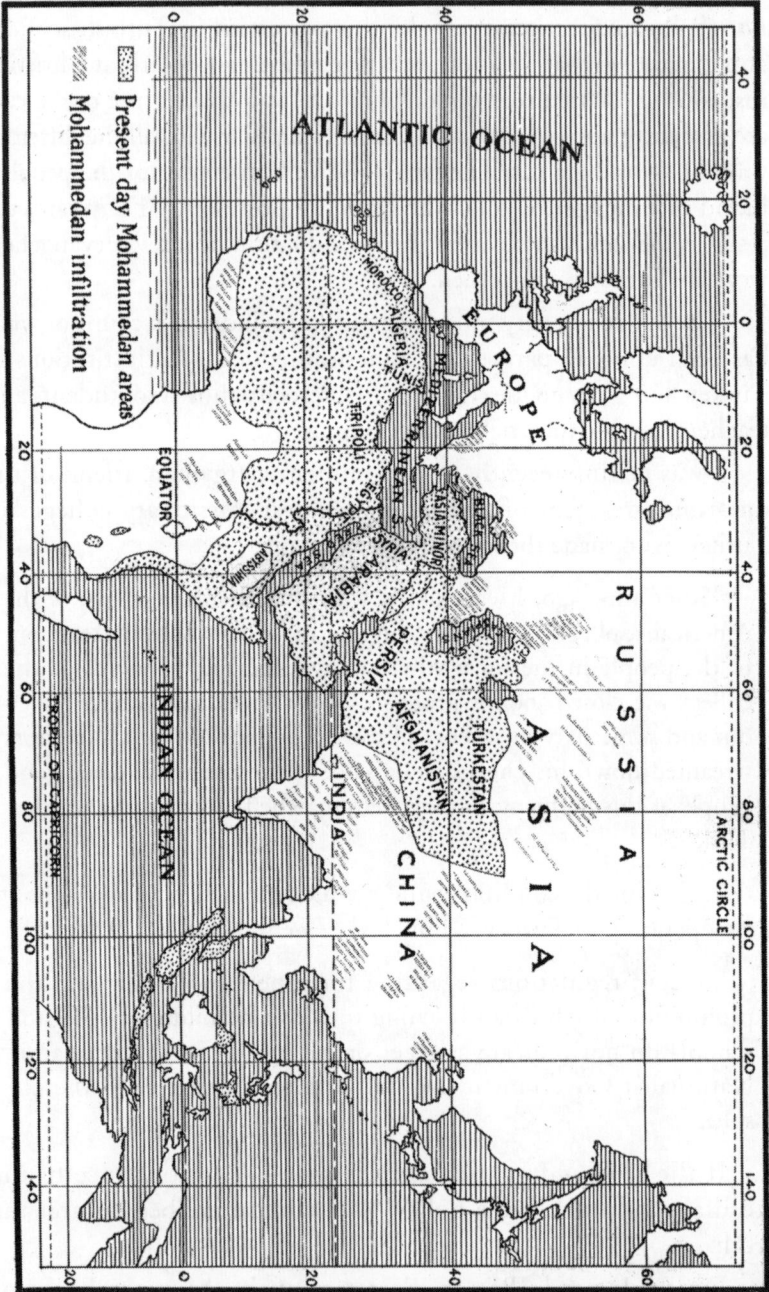

"The Present Status of Missionary and Educational Work in Turkey."

Doctor Barton is very eminent in missionary work, to which he has devoted the best part of his life, and he is naturally anxious to save as much as possible of the ruins of the magnificent edifice which the Mission Board built up in Turkey with millions of American money, and to keep going somehow. Here are some quotations from Doctor Barton's article:

"Some of the American schools have been closed because of the exchange of populations approved by the Lausanne Conference, as, for instance, Euphrates College at Harput, Central Turkey College at Aintab, Teachers' College at Sivas, and the College at Van, all in the Eastern section of Turkey are no longer in operation. These were conducted almost if not wholly for Christian students, that is, Armenians for the most part, but with a few Greeks and Syrians. Under the deportations the country was almost wholly depopulated of this part of its inhabitants. The teachers were deported or left the country so that these institutions are to-day closed. Central Turkey, which was at Aintab, however, is aiding some work in Aleppo, which is in the French mandate, to which a large number of the people of Aintab have fled, but the constituency of the other institutions are scattered far and wide.

"Anatolia College, which was at Marsovan, is in practically the same condition, although it had many Turkish students, but its teachers are scattered."

This is a very carefully worded statement and does full justice to the doctor's well-deserved reputation for diplomatic ability. There is nothing in it that might in any way offend the Turks. The general subject of the extermination of the Armenians and Greeks, and the massacre of a million of the former, the real reason of the closing of most of the schools, is obscured by reference to the "Exchange of populations approved by the Lausanne Conference."

The teachers of Anatolia College are "scattered." This is doubtless a correct expression to apply to people, many of whom have suffered martyrdom and are in Heaven, along with many of the teachers of other colleges. Let us breathe the pious wish that they are not too widely "scattered" up there, as they will certainly long to get together and talk over their experiences. Continuing, the doctor says:

"Just at the present time in the absence of regulations, the schools are hampered in their religious teaching. The Turks have given orders that there shall be no religious instruction and for the present there is nothing in the form of direct instruction during school hours and none of the students can be required to take Biblical studies or be present where religious instruction is given. Under present circumstances, it seems wise to those who are conducting schools in the Near East to comply with these regulations until a more substantial understanding can be reached and the educational system of the country be put on a sound basis"

If by a "sound basis" the doctor means—and he can not mean anything else—the permission of the Turkish Government to convert Turks in Turkey to Christianity, he will wait a long time. The "sound basis," to arrive at which the Turks have been shedding rivers of Christian blood, has already been achieved. And in the meantime, some of the Christian missionaries have accepted to cease preaching Christ. It is about time for the cock to crow. Doctor Barton continues:

"It is well known by Turks as well as by foreigners, that Turkey needs what these institutions can give, in order to enable her to organize her present administrations on a basis that would give her a worthy place in the sisterhood of nations."

When Jesus appeared to the Eleven, as they sat at meal after the Crucifixion, He enjoined them: "Go ye into all the world and preach the gospel to every creature. He that believeth and is baptized shall be saved. But he that believeth not shall be damned."

He said nothing about educating foreigners so that they could put their administrations on a sound basis. This is a laudable object but should be done and paid for by the foreigners themselves.

I am informed that the distinguished and erudite Rabbi Stephen Wise, of New York, has estimated the entire value of the American Mission property now existing in Turkey as being not more than ten million dollars. His has been one of the most eloquent voices raised in behalf of the martyred Christians in the Near East.

I wish it distinctly understood that nothing I have said is meant in any way as a reflection on American missionaries in general. I have known so many noble men and women consecrated to spreading the doctrines of the Master in foreign lands that I am incapable of saying or thinking anything derogatory of this saintly band of pioneers, or of their work. I have already described the gallant conduct of the missionary girls and men at Smyrna, and the same story has been repeated over and over in many dark corners of the globe in times of stress and danger.

I am not in sympathy with the policy of certain missionaries with regard to Turkey, and I believe that the utter failure of Christianity to direct the policy of governments, as shown in this sad narrative, renders any campaign in Moslem countries a well-nigh hopeless task. I am convinced, also, that an examination of our private lives and conduct, will convince any one that the conversion of Americans is a more crying need than that of Mohammedans.

What America needs, and what Europe needs, is a great spiritual awakening. Christ is all right. He is unutterably wonderful and lovely. Let us all unite under His banner, and then think about advancing into foreign lands.

The ruin wrought to our missionary institutions in Turkey, which has inspired so much caution with regard to the fate of the remainder, is epitomized in the following table issued in 1923 by the American Board of Foreign Missions:

Missionary Churches:	90% closed.
American Colleges:	Work suspended in six out of eight.
Hospitals:	One-half operating.
College Heads:	Two dead, one deported, three refused permission to return.
Village Schools:	(Estimated at 1000). Abandoned.
High Schools:	Only three out of forty-one now open.
Property loss:	Estimated at $2,880,000.
Native workers:	Two-thirds dead; others in exile.
Constituency:	95% dead or deported or enslaved in harems.
American Workers:	Fifty deported.

This chapter can have no more appropriate ending than the following quotation from the pen of the Reverend Ralph Harlow, formerly Missionary to Turkey, and now Professor of Biblical Literature and Comparative Religion at Smith College, Massachusetts:

"One hundred years or more ago, our fathers sent forth to Asia Minor the first American missionary. For all these years our churches have carried on the glorious task of awakening and renewing among the peoples of that land, loyalty to the person and principles of Jesus Christ. Schools and colleges, hospitals and churches have been built. A host of men and women have come to love, generation by generation, the people of that land. It was the land that gave our faith birth; it was its cradle; it planted the seed from which the church sprang in the blood of the martyrs.

"To-day the Turkish Government announces that in the future there will be no Christians in that land, and that no Protestant missionary work will be permitted." "For five hundred years, the Christians of Asia Minor have been the objects of persecution, while Christian civilization has stood by and looked on. In more recent years the barbarity of that persecution has shocked the conscience of humanity. In the eighties came the Bulgarian horrors; in the nineties came the Armenian atrocities; in 1909 Adana ran red with the blood of slaughtered thousands and echoed to the wail of countless women.

"In each case the Turk was restored to power; in each case lengthy promises of good conduct to his Christian subjects were extracted.

"From 1915 to 1918 came that series of atrocities such as the world of our day had hardly the emotions and conscience to comprehend, even amid the horror of the other cruelties of those other years. Those of us who were in the land at that time, who saw these things with our own eyes, have never told half of the truth of those dark hours. The Allied nations swore by all that was sacred, by the crosses of their fallen dead, that these things should not again be possible. One million five hundred thousand is a conservative estimate of the lives struck down in lust and torture. America sent in workers and dollars to the relief of the starving and tattered fragments of the people who survived the blast.

"The man most responsible for all this horror was Talaat Bey. What is the attitude of the government of Mustapha Khemal to Talaat and his methods? When Talaat died the government at Angora held a service in his honor. The *Yeni Gun,* the official organ of the Nationalist party, came out with great mourning bands of black. In the editorial were these sentences: 'Talaat wrote the most glorious pages in Turkish history. Let the eyes that do not weep become blind. Let the heart that does not ache cease to beat.' Khemal has followed in the footsteps of Talaat. Massacres, deportations, cruelty, outrage and terror, have marked the reign of the Nationalist government. The Smyrna tragedy has taken place in hundreds of villages on a smaller scale. The innocence of childhood, the sacredness of womanhood, the tears of mothers, the cries of the helpless, make no appeal at all to the armies or the courts of this government."

Chapter 32

THE REVEREND RALPH HARLOW
ON THE LAUSANNE TREATY

IN proof of the statement that many eminent followers of Christ are not in entire sympathy with certain missionaries in their policy with regard to the Turks, I am quoting again from the Reverend Ralph Barlow. The following extracts are from an article and two letters written by him. The article appeared in the *Outlook* of October 25, 1922, and in it, among other things, the author describes an interview with the late Theodore Roosevelt:

> "At that time, I had just returned from Asia Minor where I had witnessed the fearful deportations on the Bagdad Railroad, and could give him first-hand information of the awful atrocities going on. He asked me a number of questions, continually shaking his head and saying, 'terrible, terrible, terrible.'

> "Then with a tense expression on his face, he said, 'Mr. Barlow, the greatest regret that I have as I look back on my administration is the fact that when the awful Adana massacre occurred, this government did not take steps against the outrage on civilization!' "

A further quotation from the same article indicates that the men on destroyers did not fully share the pro-Turk sentiments of their officers:

> "I have just listened to the contents of a letter sent by one of our boys on an American destroyer at Smyrna. He tells of having to stand by while the brutal Turkish soldiers seized beautiful Christian girls and tore them screaming from their mothers and outraged them right on the public quay of Smyrna. He saw these brutal soldiers shooting down helpless women with children in their arms, unarmed men beaten to death by the butts of these Turkish soldiery. And then he tells of the anguish that he felt because the orders of our government were such that he had to stand by, helpless, before such atrocities."

American Consular Building, Smyrna, before which Turkish soldiers poured inflammable liquids. It was completely consumed.

I have been told that many such letters were written by our navy boys at Smyrna to relatives and friends in the United States. In a letter to me, Mr. Barlow says that he believes it to be his duty to tell the truth about affairs in the Near East, and he continues:

"Doctor MacLachlan and Reed demanded my resignation and said that I endangered the college. I resigned. I have been made to feel that I ought to keep still, but justice seems to me greater than buildings and institutions. At the time of the Lausanne Conference and after, I claimed that our American Board (of Foreign Missions) ought to have stood four square against the wretched treaty. Dr. Barton did not like the openness of my criticisms and I lost a position as Board Secretary through his opposition to me."

The second letter referred to gives Mr. Barlow's opinion of the Lausanne Treaty and is addressed to the Reverend Doctor Barton, Foreign Secretary of the American Board of Foreign Missions. As some of the missionaries who are desirous of saving the remnants of their installations in Turkey have come out in favor of the treaty, Mr. Barlow's opinion on the subject, and his reasons, may be of interest:

"At the time of the conference, and following it, I was asked to discuss the situation in numerous addresses, so that I read up carefully everything I could get which would throw light on the subject. All the evidence goes to show that the men who went to Lausanne were influenced from the very first in all their decisions to protect the oil interests, which featured largely behind the scenes in the Conference discussions. That those interests were so strong as to overshadow the humanitarian and missionary interests I have accepted without question, until I read your paragraph.

"I turn now to some of my sources of information, for which you ask. Unfortunately, most of my material on this subject is in my files at Northampton, but I have with me references, which will perhaps indicate why I have associated oil with blood in connection with Lausanne. I would refer you to the following articles and I might name numerous others: 'American Blood and Oil,' *Literary Digest*, December 30, 1922; 'Oil and Glory at Lausanne,' *Literary Digest*, July 28, 1923; 'Blind Forces at Lausanue,' *Asia*, April, 1923; 'Britain's Mesopotamian Burden and Oil,' *Literary Digest*, December 15, 1922; 'Issues at Lausanue,' *Living Age*, January 6, 1923; 'Lausanne and its Antecedents,' *Fortnightly Review*, January, 1923; 'Uncle Sam Mixing in the Turkish Broil,' *Literary Digest*, December

23, 1922; 'The Tragedy of Lausanne, *Association Men,* March or April, 1923; 'The World Race for Oil,' *Literary Digest,* January 20, 1923.

"If you will take the time and trouble, as I have, to read even these few articles, and the "Literary Digest" quotes from many other sources, you will find that the main theme is that the humanitarian interests at Lausanne were sold out, because of oil interests, and that the missionary interests got no-where.

"A regular official of the Standard Oil came to Lausanne before the Conference opened. Lewis Heck, who was in the business in Constantinople came to Lausanne as a member of the American delegation.[*]

"Young MacDowell, who had many railroad concessions in Turkey which dovetailed into the Chester concessions, was in Beck's Constantinople office. Heck knows Turkey well. I will be willing to defend the thesis that the entire course of events, which made the Lausanne Treaty possible, was determined by the ambitions of the commercial oil interests, and that, in this race for Turkish favors, the Americans led the way."

Mr. Barlow quotes many editorials and articles in the American and British press, the general tenor of which can be gleaned from one or two examples:

"Lausanne was all that an International Conference ought not to be. It was the sacrifice of all human and humanitarian questions to expediency." *New York Journal of Commerce,* July, 1923.

"Mosul and freedom to give us a chance in the scramble for oil has been the object of all the negotiations, but the United States might be better occupied to-day than looking after the interests of oil kings. Peace and civilization may be talked about in public, but in private there is talk of oil, because territories where the future concessionaires will be at pains to insure their rights, are at stake." *New York Times.*

"Although America would accept no humane responsibility in the Near East, saying that it must be free from troubles and depravities of the Old World, America's blood boils over the burning question of oil. When the word 'oil' is mentioned, the recluse bursts from its

---

[*] Lewis Heck had been closely associated with the Chester interests, and Admiral Chester's son was also at Lausanne.—R.H.

retirement upon the instant. America has no concern with Asia Minor while the Turk butchers his Christian subjects by the hundreds of thousands." *Pall Mall Gazette.*

Chapter 33

MOHAMMEDANISM AND CHRISTIANITY

IT is difficult for Americans, living in this Christian country, to understand the position of a missionary who goes into a Mohammedan community with the intention of converting its members.

The problem is exactly that which would confront a Moslem hodja, or priest, should he appear with two or three veiled wives in a devout Methodist community in Michigan and open up a campaign in behalf of the Prophet. As for the results of education upon a Mohammedan, whenever he is made to doubt his own religion, when he is educated out of it, he generally becomes an atheist. The spectacle of the Great War has profoundly influenced all non-Christian peoples and has made missionary work more difficult than ever. "Christ is not the Prince of Peace," they say; and no amount of preaching can make them believe it. "Prince of Peace," they sneer, "He is the Prince of the submarine, the bomb-throwing aeroplane, poison gas, the machine gun." The supposed results of the teachings of Christ are more evident than the teachings themselves. One element of strength of the Mohammedan religion is that it is sincere and gives free play to the passions and impulses of man's lower nature. Whatever the teachings of the Koran as to spreading its doctrines by the sword—for the interpreters of that sacred book are legion, and one may find anything he wishes in it—there is no doubt as to the example set by Mohammed, who founded his kingdom sword in hand, who was a polygamist, a robber of camel caravans and gave orders for the assassination of his enemies. This is not said in a spirit of defamation of the Prophet, but as a statement of well-known historic facts. While advocating many virtues, the Koran gives more play to the human passions and makes a greater appeal to the natural man than the asceticism of Christianity and hence spreads more rapidly among primitive peoples and those of a lower grade of civilization.

I once met a sweet missionary woman returning from Africa with her little child, who had fallen sick of fever, to America for medical treatment. She described the great advance of Mohammedanism in Africa and the seemingly hopeless task of the Christian missionaries there. She made a sort of map of mission stations and explained: "We are trying to put a barrier across Africa to prevent Mohammedanism spreading to the South, beyond the equator," "From what you say to me," I observed, "you can not do it." "We can't," she said, "but God can." This seems unanswerable and must appeal strongly to the religious devotee, but there is an answer and it is this: "God can, of course He can; but He doesn't, and probably He will not." It seems probable that the great gift of Christianity has been so abused and shamed by the so-called Christian nations that God is weary of them, and considers it presumptuous for them to send out missionaries to convert people of another faith. It has been abundantly shown to all reasonable human beings, who are not religious zealots, that money expended in the attempt to convert Moslems is money thrown away. Even the missionaries themselves in Turkey seem to have given it up.

The same story is heard everywhere. In *The Crescent in Northwest China,* by G. Findlay Andrew, a missionary, the author says: "Islam has often been referred to as the challenge to Christian missions. During the past few years a few Hwei-Hwei (Chinese Moslems) have been reached with the Gospel and, after a profession of faith, have been accepted as church members or as inquirers. The number has, however, been very small, and of those who have 'kept the faith' only about one remains in church fellowship at the time of writing." And yet the good missionary sums this gloomy report up with the remark: "Great as the problem is, yet the triumph of the Cross over the Crescent in Kansu is assured." It is difficult to follow the process of reasoning which derives this conclusion from these premises.

The attention of the reader has already been called to the fact that the Turks are the lowest of the Moslem races and it would not be fair to Mohammedans in general to say that they approve of butchery and rape as carried out by that people, so well characterized by Gladstone and many historians. In fact the Turks are not the greatest danger to the Christian church. They have accomplished their fell task, and their influence as a proselytizing power will not spread beyond their own dominions unless they wage another successful war.

A few quotations from that penetrating book, *The New World of Islam,* by Lothrop Stoddard, will suffice to show how Islamism is ousting Christianity in those places where it meets it face to face. The strongest and best organized proselytizing order among the Moslems are the Senussiya, well described by Mr. Stoddard:

"The beginning of systematic, self-conscious pan-Islamism dates from about the middle of the nineteenth century. The Sennussi are careful to avoid a downright breach with European Powers. Their long-headed, cautious policy is truly astonishing. For more than half a century the order has been a great force, yet it has never risked the supreme adventure. In many of the fanatic risings, which have occurred in various parts of Africa, local Sennussi have undoubtedly taken part, and the same was true during the Italian campaign in Tripoli and the late war, but the order itself has never officially entered the lists. The Sennussi program is the welding, first, of Moslem Africa, and, later of the whole Moslem world into the revived "Imamat," of Islam's early days; into a great theocracy embracing all true believers—in other words, pan-Islamism. But they believe that the political liberation of Islam from Christian domination must be preceded by a profound spiritual regeneration. Year after year and decade after decade the Sennussi advance slowly, calmly, coldly. They are covering North Africa with their lodges and schools; and to the southward converting millions of pagan Negroes to the faith of Islam. Every candid European observer tells the same story. As an Englishman remarked some twenty years ago: 'Mohammedanism is making remarkable progress in the interior of Africa. It is crushing Paganism out. Against it the Christian propaganda is a myth.' And a French protestant missionary remarks in the same vein: 'We see Islam on its march, sometimes slowed down, but never stopped, toward the heart of Africa. It fears nothing. Even Christianity, its most serious rival, it views without hate. While Christians dream of the conquest of Africa, Mohammedans do it.' These gains are being made at the expense of African Christianity as well. The European missions lose many of their converts to Islam, while across the continent, the ancient Abyssinian Church, so long an outpost against Islam, seems in danger of submersion by the rising Moslem tide. There is to-day in the Moslem world a wide spread conviction that Islam is entering on a period of Renaissance and renewed glory."

Mohammedanism to-day covers the northern part of Africa from the Atlantic Ocean to the Red Sea, nearly to the equator, far below which it has passed on the East; it surrounds Abyssinia, an island of degenerate Christianity; it holds solidly Arabia, Persia, Afghanistan, Turkostan and has overrun large portions of China and Russia, where it is making rapid progress. It is one of the leading religions of India, and has reached the Dutch Indies and Philippines.

Pierre Andre, in his work *Islam et les Races,* gave the total number of Mohammedans in the world in 1917, as 246,920,000; Laurence Martin of the Library of Congress, in an article in *Foreign Affairs* for March, 1923, gives the total number as 230,000,000, a slightly more conservative figure; but any estimate must be revised yearly, as the number is increasing with astounding rapidity. It is probable that the number of Mohammedans in the world to-day is about 250,000,000.

To the above vast portions of the earth's surface which have already been mentioned as solidly Mohammedan must now be added Asia Minor, the last hope and outpost of Christian civilization in the Near East, which was rapidly spreading and developing with the aid of our own and other Christian schools, but which has recently been cleared out by fire and massacre with the aid and connivance of the Christian powers.

It has already been asserted that conversions from Mohammedanism to Christianity are extremely rare, while the former is taking heavy toll from Christian converts. It seems also that there are well-authenticated cases of Europeans and Americans having embraced Islam. Professor T. W. Arnold in his ingenious defense of Mohammedanism, *The Preaching of Islam,* cites the case of an English solicitor, Mr. William Henry Quillam, who embraced Mohammedanism and became a missionary of that faith in the city of Liverpool. By 1897, ten years after his own conversion, Mr. Quillam had made one hundred and thirty-seven proselytes.

An American, Mr. Alexander Russell Webb, at one time United States Consul to Manila, after having embraced Mohammedanism, opened a mission. Mr. Webb had been brought up as a Presbyterian. In 1875, a Methodist preacher named Norman became converted to Mohammedanism and began to preach it in America.

While I was in Smyrna a native-born American, who was weary of a devoutly Christian and ascetic wife, so good that he could not get a divorce from her, became a Mohammedan in order to marry a young woman with whom he had fallen in love, and with whom he was living happily, as man and wife according to Mohammedan law, up until quite recently. There is also the well-authenticated story, which, for obvious reasons, has not been given wide publicity, of the American missionary woman who married a rich Turk and became a member of his already well-stocked harem. A number of her former associates went to see her and endeavored to persuade her to return to them. She replied:

"I have always desired to be married and live the natural life of a woman, for which God intended me. I saw the years slipping away, with no chance in sight of fulfilling the functions for which the Creator made me and I rebelled. No Christian man has ever made me an honorable proposal of marriage, though several have paid me court with shady intentions. This man offered me a union honorable according to his religion and the laws of the country, and I accepted. I would rather have a quarter of a man than none at all. I am soon to become a mother; I am perfectly happy, and I don't want ever to hear anything more about missionaries or missionary work."

The two last cases are significant as they reveal one of the reasons why Mohammedanism is less difficult to preach convincingly, under favorable conditions, than Christianity. It solves, both for men and women, some of the inconveniences of our civilization, which exist despite the greater and greater efficiency of our divorce courts.

These pages are written without any spirit of fanaticism and with the sole object of giving the world, especially the Christian world, the truth about certain matters of great historic significance. The Mohammedans, in the organized propaganda which they are making against Christianity, both by written arguments and by their extensive system of lay missionaries, are well aware of the unchristian history of the Christian world, and the fearful spectacle of the Great War has added a powerful argument to their already full quiver. They are aware also that the teachings of Christ, while never having dictated to any great extent the policies of governments, have also failed to regulate as they should the lives of individuals. Mohammedanism does not ask so much of the individual as does Christianity, and hence is easier to live up to. There is consequently less hypocrisy. For instance, the marriage relation is very lax in the Prophet's creed and polygamy is permitted. A Mohammedan writer says that the social evil is unknown in Mohammedan countries, and a writer in *Armenia,* the defunct Boston periodical of that name, replies that this is true for the reason that the Moslem is permitted by his religion to make his own home a brothel. The Moslem propaganda argues that their various women have an open and honorable standing, while the Christian has illicit relations, which frequently ruin his victims, whom he abandons to a life of dishonor.

But we are approaching the Mohammedan in the matter of loose marriage relations, and in the need of missionary work at home. In 1922, more than one out of every eight married couples were divorced in the United States, and it is frequent with us to have a succession of partners, rivaling the Mohammedan in this particular. In 1922 there were 184,554 divorces in the United States, as against 112,036 in 1916. In 1922 there were fifty-two lynchings in the United States. In 1922 there were 4,931,905 illiterates in this country, and in the same year a percentage that reached nearly twenty-three of illiteracy among the Negroes of seven Southern States.[*]

The Koran does not permit the use of wine, and devout Mohammedans abstain from the use of intoxicants. In the United States the Constitution is very generally violated by large masses of the population and the day of Christ's Nativity is largely celebrated by drunken orgies. Secret vice is prevalent in the United States to a much larger extent than many people dream of. Every few days some automobile overturns, killing a guilty couple, or some girl, in fear of the vice inspector, jumps out of a window, revealing depravity in circles where it was least expected.

Christianity lost her power as a world-conquering religion—and thus became an easy prey to Mohammedanism—as soon as she became obscured in a smoke-screen of controversy. The innumerable and bewildering quibbles which arose, giving rise to many sects, and the violent hatreds and schisms engendered, form a history in themselves. At the time when Mohammed appeared on the scene, the Church was already split into quarreling sects, who had lost sight of the simple teachings of the Master. Christians had become depraved and general immorality and degeneracy were rife.

---

[*] *A Survey of Southern Illiteracy,* published by the Education Board, Southern Baptist Convention, Birmingham, 1923.

To-day the Christian world is about evenly divided between Protestants and Catholics, rival sects, showing little spirit of compromise. Recent statistics, given by *Whittaker's Almanac,* place the total number of Catholics in the world at 272,860,000 and of Protestants and other denominations, (like the Eastern Church), who deny the jurisdiction of the Pope, at 290,000,000. Any one who has lived for any time in countries where missionaries are active will testify to the saintly character of Catholic Sisters, and the devotion of the Brothers. They will equally bear witness to the high character, courage and beauty of life of Protestant missionaries, men and women. But the two sects are antagonistic.

In Smyrna during the Greek administration, a Y.M.C.A. was started and was doing excellent work, as also a Y.W.C.A. A notice was posted in all the Catholic churches that such institutions were of darkness and not of light and that all true Christians must keep away from them. A Catholic teacher in the Y.W.C.A. who was being paid a good salary and who needed it was compelled to resign her post. This is but one instance of many that could be given. When a Mohammedan is asked to be a Christian, a common answer is, "What kind? There are so many kinds of you, each warning us against the others." There is less hope to-day of pan-Christianity than of pan-Islamism. Says Kurtz, already referred to: "To-day Mohammedanism is the one rival of Christianity to become a world religion," and a writer in the *Moslem World* for January, 1925: "The Christian Church, after thirteen centuries of hard struggle finds Islam still a most baffling problem. It is true historically that Islam has been born after Christianity and has displaced it almost wherever it has spread. The history of the whole of North Africa, Palestine and Syria, and present Asia Minor shows this plainly."

The Reverend George Bush in his *Life of Mohammed,* published by the Harpers in 1830, makes the following reflection:

"Indeed in this, as in every other instance where the fortunes of an individual are entirely disproportionate to the means employed, and surpass all reasonable calculation, we are forced to resolve the problem into the special Providence of God. Nothing short of this could have achieved such mighty results."

If there is no other explanation of Mohammedan success, it is evident that the Divine intention has not varied in the last ninety years. This is the viewpoint of the deeply religious man, who believes in God's personal management of all the affairs of this world, attributing to reasons of Divine wisdom matters too deep for human penetration. The student of history will understand the spread of Mohammedanism at the expense of Christianity, and the chief reasons have appeared or will become plain in the course of this narrative.

A stouter and more virile figure than Mohammed attempted to establish a similar creed on this continent. He failed to become a world influence, a permanent factor in history, for geographical reasons, mainly. The part of the world in which Brigham Young planted his polygamous creed was not so well adapted to its expansion as the scene of Mohammed's early activities. Western civilization, following close on the heels of the gold rush, overwhelmed the American apostle and intimate of the Angel Gabriel. The chief reason why Christianity has lost so much ground before Mohammedanism, and is likely to lose much more, is that there has never been much *real* Christianity in the world.

The history of the so-called "Christian Nations" has been a long tale of bloody wars, of treachery and robbery, of St. Bartholomew Days and of Catholics martyrized by Protestants; of persecutions, of saints and witches burned at the stake.

And the situation among the "Christian Nations" that allowed the Turks to burn Smyrna and massacre and abuse its inhabitants was such a culmination of infamy and shame as shows that the world is becoming less Christian as the years go by.

Surely there is no reason to expect God to aid Christian missionaries, after such a disappointment and travesty. If, as the Reverend Bush remarks, the wonderful spread of Mohammedanism can only be explained as some special Providence of God, He may be inspiring the Sennussi to spiritualize their religion and develop the better features of it. If the Christian faith has had so feeble effect upon the conduct of Christian nations and has so little harmony that it lacks the force to convert Mohammedans, then the only alternative open to wisdom, finite or infinite, would be to make the best of some other creed. When our missionaries have finished putting the Turkish administrations "on a sound basis," they might come home and teach us to be better Christians. Unless Christianity is saved in those countries where it still has a nominal existence, it is doomed, and their civilization will go with it. The Bolsheviks understand this, as witness the war they are waging against religion.

Chapter 34

THE KORAN AND THE BIBLE

THE peculiar state of mind which has enabled the Turk to commit outrages on humanity that have shocked and insulted the entire race have been due to three things: his own nature, the teachings of the Koran and the example of the Prophet. This is what Gladstone means when he speaks of the "combination of his nature and his religion."

This is better understood when we take into consideration that other branches of the Mohammedans have made great contributions to the progress and culture of the world. The Arabs have distinguished themselves in architecture, science, poetry, art and letters. It is the opinion of that distinguished churchman, Canon William Barry, expressed in an article in *The Nineteenth Century and After* for August, 1919, that other Moslems should repudiate the Turk and his outrages. Canon Barry says:

"Wise Moslems, instead of being stirred up in defense of a system condemned by history and experience, should be led to perceive in the Turk, not any 'Bulwark of Islam,' but a stain upon their civilization, a lapse from the glory of their illustrious Caliphs, a scandal and a weakness not to be endured any more."

In support of this, one has only to hark back to the splendid days of Bagdad and Cordova.

In the days of Haroun al Raschid, Bagdad was renowned as the greatest city in the world, a center of refinement, learning and art. This monarch is described as having gathered about him a brilliant company of poets, jurists, learned men and wits. That civilization has left behind one classic, which has immortalized it—even though it naively treats of a monarch who had a new wife every night whose head he cut off in the morning.

But here we have the same old story: Bagdad fell into insignificance after it came under the sway of the Turks; and at the time of its final capture in 1638 by the Sultan Murad IV, that monarch massacred most of its inhabitants, contrary to the terms of capitulation.

The Moors have left behind them in Spain monuments of architecture, which are to this day a delight to the world; we have only to cite the Mosque—now the Cathedral—at Cordova, and the Alhambra of Grenada. The famous Algebra of Omar Khayyám was written in Arabic and many contributions to science and literature have first appeared in that language. The Arab of Africa is described by travelers as the noblest specimen, physically, of the human race, and even the casual tourist who has touched at Algiers, has confirmed this fact by observation of the men in its streets. The difference, mentally, between the Arab and the Turk, is thus depicted by Buckhardt:

"The Arab displays his manly character when he defends his guest at the peril of his own life and submits to the reverses of fortune, to disappointment and distress with the most patient resignation. He is distinguished from the Turk by the virtues of pity and gratitude. The Turk is cruel, the Arab is of a more kindly temper; he pities and supports the wretched and never forgets the generosity shown him even by an enemy."

Without having gone deeply into the subject, I am convinced that the Turks are the only branch of the Mohammedan faith, which has never made any contributions to the progress of civilization or produced anything which, as Sir Edwin Pears says, "the world would gladly keep." They have been destructive and not constructive.

To understand how human beings could have developed such traits of ferocity and have left such a record of massacres, and for the benefit of those who believe that a high state of civilization is now to be built up by these people, who have definitely rejected the teachings of Christ, let us cast a glance at the comparative doctrines of the Koran and the Bible.

That the teachings of the New Testament are infinitely more softening and uplifting than those of the Koran, no one can deny after a brief and intelligent comparative study. The general spirit of the latter book—and the statement is made despite the contention of those commentators who hold the contrary—is that of spreading its doctrines and the power and dominion of its followers by the sword; to destroy the unbeliever or make him pay tribute. It is polygamous in its teachings.

It is founded on the Old Testament and in it appear the chief historical characters of that book. It is completed, or rounded out, by much of Oriental fable and belief in supernatural beings, such as the Jinns of the *Arabian Nights;* to which are added the so-called *Revelations of the Prophet.* Some of these are merely for the purpose of allowing Mohammed to gratify his own desires, as, for instance, the case in which one of his friends is commanded by the angel to give his beautiful wife to the Prophet.

A great literature of commentary has grown up around the Koran, and it would be possible for its defenders to find much in it preaching tolerance, but its general effect upon its disciples, combined with the example of the Prophet's life, convincingly prove that Mohammedanism is a creed to be spread by the sword. Written originally in Arabic, it is claimed for it that its beauties can only be appreciated in that language and that the lines in which it is composed make a peculiar appeal to its readers and linger in the memory.

This contention can only be understood, of course, by those who are versed in the Arabic. It was for a similar reason that *Tupper's Proverbial Philosophy* was at one time universally popular. I have read the New Testament in the original Greek, in Latin, French, English and portions of it in German and Swedish and I am competent to state that the words of Christ lend themselves to translation because of the beauty and value of the thought intrinsically, and because of the universal appeal, in every age, which it contains.

The Sermon on the Mount is as overwhelmingly touching and irresistible in English, French or German, as it is in the original Greek. The same may be said of the Lord's Prayer, and of most of the words of the Master. This is why, when Christianity is blotted out of vast areas of the earth's surface by the sword, the club, by the ax and fire, we can consider that the world has retrograded for some thousands of years in those regions, and that the interests of the race have in general been irretrievably injured, no matter who gets the concessions.

The New Testament advocates purity of life and even leans toward asceticism. Christ himself was unmarried and was of spotless purity. The Koran is sensual in its teachings, both as to this life and the life hereafter. It promises the true believer an allotment of paradisiacal females when he arrives in the other world. What the relation of the earthly wives will be to this new group is more or less uncertain. This doctrine of the Koran throws the light very clearly on the contemptuous regard, in which woman is held by the followers of Mohammed.

Such a lofty, pure and beautiful Idyl, as the life and death of Lord Tennyson and his lady, is not possible to a creed of polygamy and heavenly houries. Heaven is thus described in the Koran:

> "Therein shall receive them lovely damsels refraining their eyes from beholding any but their spouses, whom no man shall have touched before, neither any spirit (Jinn) and having complexions like rubies and pearls."

In connection with this, one must remember that Mohammedans hold the Koran in deep reverence and believe it literally. Among the great mass of them, there is not that advanced thought and development of education which might cause them to regard skeptically their sacred book, as is the case among Christians. When a Mohammedan dies on the field of battle he actually believes that he is going straight to a beautiful garden where a bevy of voluptuous females await him.

According to the Koran, divorce is easy and can be obtained by the husband simply proclaiming that he is weary of his spouse. The wife, on the other hand, can only obtain divorce for sufficient causes. In fact, matrimonial ties in Mohammedan countries are flimsy. No better example of the ease of Mohammedan divorce can be given, than that of Mustapha Khemal, the Turkish leader, and his wife. The American papers explained that Khemal himself pronounced the decree, his priestly functions enabling him so to do; but the fact is that divorce in Mohammedan countries is an extremely simple process for both high and low.

The Koran teaches non-indulgences in wine, and in general devout believers are absolutely tee-toddlers. The cultivation of grape and the making of wine does not prevail among the followers of Mohammed.

Circumcision, non-eating of pork, objection to statues and photographs, are all borrowed from the Old Testament, the last named from the commandment, "Thou shalt not make to thyself any graven image."

Scene on railroad pier, Smyrna, where refugees embarked.

Not one Turk in a thousand, if that many, can read the Koran, as it is written in Archaic Arabic, but the general conception that they are the faithful and all others are "dogs of unbelievers" is well fixed in their minds as also the few broad articles of faith hitherto enumerated. Illiteracy is generally prevalent among the Turkish people, and the hodjas or priests do not do much in the way of teaching except crying from the minarets "God is God and Mahomet is His Prophet." Nevertheless, during the horrible days of massacre, fire and rape in Smyrna, the Turks were chanting, with joy: "Their wives shall be widows and their children orphans." Hearing this, and thinking of the thousands of babes who were being made fatherless, or subjected to suffering and death, I could not help remembering the words: "Suffer the little children to come unto me, for of such is the Kingdom of Heaven."

Mr. Geddes in his statement asserts that in no instance did he see any Moslem giving alms to Armenians, it being a criminal offense for any one to aid them, the object of the deportations being "the extermination of the race." The teachings of the Mohammedan cult render it possible to issue such an order to an entire nation, with the certainty that it will be universally obeyed.

Chapter 35

THE EXAMPLE OF MOHAMMED

THOUGH there have been great Mohammedan civilizations that have contributed much to the world's progress and have left imperishable monuments, they have not lasted. They have arisen through the fundamentally noble character and intelligence of the peoples that have founded them, and have flourished for a relatively short time rather in spite of their creed than because of it. And, as is the case in all religions, the example set by the originator has had a greater influence on his disciples than his book. The Prophet is deeply reverenced by all Mohammedans, who regard even one hair from his beard as having miraculous power.

The main facts of his life and his general character are known to them. These salient facts will now be set forth without bias of hostility or irreverence. They are authentic and well established. The reader is invited to confirm them and determine for himself whether or not they are correctly stated:

1. Mohammed was a polygamist;

2. After leaving Mecca and proceeding to Mesina, where he established himself for a time, he organized and conducted raids against caravans, which he robbed to replenish his depleted treasury;

3. He besieged and plundered towns for the booty, which acts he justified by "revelations";

4. He ordered eight hundred Jewish prisoners to be separated from their wives and children and butchered and their bodies thrown into a trench. Their wives and families were sold into captivity. This was the first Mohammedan massacre.[*]

5. He ordered ferocious and inhuman punishments to be inflicted;[†]

6. He removed his enemies by murder and assassination.

We have seen how faithfully this example has been followed by the Turks throughout the years, since the fall of Constantinople, and especially by the Young Turks since their accession to power. But

---

[*] Draycatt, *Mahomet*, page 234 et sq.
[†] Draycott, 253–254.

although other branches of the Mohammedan race have shown conspicuous qualities of heart and of head, yet a general study of the spread of that religion from its inception reveals only too clearly the influence of the Prophet's example as well as of his teachings. Says Pears, already quoted:

"The history indeed, of Egypt, of Syria and of Asia Minor had been a long series of massacres, culminating perhaps in that of Egypt where in 1354, when the Christians were ordered to abjure their faith and accept Mohammedanism and refused, a hundred thousand were put to death."

Adrian Fortescue, in his work, *The Lesser Eastern Churches,* has this paragraph:

"In 1389, a great procession of Copts who had accepted Mohammed under fear of death, marched through Cairo. Repenting of their apostasy, they now wished to atone for it by the inevitable consequence of returning to Christianity. So as they marched, they announced that they believed in Christ and renounced Mohammed. They were seized and all the men were beheaded in an open square before the women. But this did not terrify the women; so they, too, were all martyred."

Regarding the Armenian massacres of our own time, Doctor Johannes Lepsius, to whose masterly *Secret Report* reference has been made in earlier pages, makes the following statement:

"We have lists before us of 550 villages whose surviving inhabitants were converted to Islam with fire and sword; of 568 churches thoroughly pillaged, destroyed and razed to the ground; of 282 Christian churches transformed into mosques; of 21 Protestant preachers and 170 Gregorian (Armenian) who were, after enduring unspeakable tortures, murdered after their refusal to accept Islam. We repeat, however, that these figures reach only to the extent of our information, and do not by a long way reach to the extent of the reality. Is this a religious persecution or is it not?"

Christianity, then, has been cleaned out of North Africa and the old Byzantine Empire, the home of the early Fathers of the Church and of the Seven Cities, largely by massacre; the Turk, when he burned Smyrna and made Asia Minor solidly Mohammedan, finished a work that has been going on for centuries.

Not only have these methods been used for propagating Mohammedanism, but the "Law of Apostates" prescribes death, forced separation from wife and family, and loss of property and legal rights for any Moslem who forsakes his faith and adheres to another. The fear of these dreadful punishments is one of the reasons why there are so few converts from Mohammedanism to Christianity. Doctor Samuel M. Zwemmer, the learned writer on Mohammedan matters, gives many examples of the application of this law in his recent work, *The Law of Apostasy in Islam*.

An example which came within my personal observation, the murder of the convert of the International College at Smyrna, has already been referred to. This is probably the same case as that cited by the Reverend Ralph Harlow, one time pastor of the International College at Smyrna, in a pamphlet: "Outside the Walls of Smyrna his body was found, stabbed in many places."

The Law of Apostasy, according to Zwemmer, is signed up by the Mohammedan law-givers in the following words:

"As for Apostates, it is permitted to kill them by facing them or coming upon them from behind, just as in the case of Polytheists. Secondly, their blood, if shed, brings no vengeance. Thirdly, their property is the spoil of true believers. Fourthly, their marriage ties become null and void."

The educated, Europeanized Turk of Constantinople is a shrewd and polished gentleman of seductive manners; but one thing must never be forgotten by those interested, financially or otherwise, in the future of Turkey; that country has been made "homogeneous" by a series of ferocious massacres carefully planned and relentlessly carried out by just such polished and seductive gentlemen, who have exploited Moslem fanaticism for their purposes, and it is on that fanaticism that their power rests.

Chapter 36

THE "50–50" THEORY

ONE OF the cleverest statements circulated by the Turkish propagandists is to the effect that the massacred Christians were as bad as their executioners, that it was "50–50." This especially appeals strongly to the Anglo-Saxon sense of justice, relieves one of all further annoyance or responsibility, and quiets the conscience. But it requires a very thoughtless person indeed to accept such a statement, and extremely little thought required to show the fallacy of it.

In the first place, the Christians in the power of the Turk have never had much opportunity to massacre, even had they been so disposed. If a few Turks have been killed in the long history of butcheries that have soaked the empire with blood, the reckoning, mathematically, will not be 50–50, nor even one to ten thousand. In addition to this, even with the shortcomings of the Christians of the world, in general, the teachings of Christ have made it better. In all the former Ottoman provinces that have succeeded in casting off the Turkish blight—Hungary, Bulgaria, Serbia, Greece—there is very little, if any, record of Turks massacred by Christians.

The conduct of the Greeks toward the thousands of Turks residing in Greece, while the ferocious massacres were going on, and while Smyrna was being burned and refugees, wounded, outraged and ruined, were pouring into every port of Hellas, was one of the most inspiring and beautiful chapters in all that country's history. There were no reprisals. The Turks living in Greece were in no wise molested, nor did any storm of hatred or revenge burst upon their heads. This is a great and beautiful victory that, in its own way, rises to the level of Marathon and Salamis.

One naturally asks what other Christian nation could have done any better? In fact, the whole conduct of Greece, during and after the persecution of the Christians in Turkey, has been most admirable, as witness also its treatment of the Turkish prisoners of war, and its efforts for the thousands of refugees that have been thrown upon its soil. I know of what I am speaking, for I was in Greece and saw with my own eyes. No one, I think, will have the courage to dispute these facts.

Had the Greeks, after the massacres in the Pontus and at Smyrna, massacred all the Turks in Greece, the record would have been 50–50—almost.

Chapter 37

ASIA MINOR, THE GRAVEYARD
OF GREEK CITIES

THE possibilities of Asia Minor for Aryan civilization are better understood when one casts an eye back on that country to the period when it was covered with teeming millions and dotted with cities that were mothers of art, literature, philosophy, industry and all that is most useful and beautiful in human development. All this has been repeatedly swept over by Asiatic and Mongol invasion and is now covered with the Turkish blight.

In a paper read in December, 1922, by W. H. Buckler, of Baltimore, the well-known diplomat and archeologist, he calls attention to the great wealth of opportunity for archeological research in New Turkey, and he urges American scholars to concentrate their attention upon Anatolia and its new capital, Angora, and he expects that "the development of towns, roads, etc., will be much more rapid than formerly, and this change will be most marked at Angora, which, from a village must shortly transform herself into a metropolis."

It is possible that a few new buildings may be put up at Angora in the near future, but the process of reasoning which connects the carrying out of massacres on a hitherto unprecedented scale with a freshly acquired ability for administration, agriculture, commerce and finance is incomprehensible.

On this point, precisely, Sir Valentine Chirol, already quoted, very opportunely says:

"The Turk's only real business was, and always has been, war. But it is difficult to see how far Turkey has profited by exchanging a narrow religious fanaticism for an equally narrow racial fanaticism. All we need consider is what Turkey is to-day. Her population is estimated at between six million and eight million decimated by the war and believed to be shrinking as it was already doing before the war, from congenital disease. It will, it is true, be for the first time, an almost purely Turkish population, for of the Greeks and Armenians who in 1914 still numbered some three million in Asia Minor, only the scantiest remnants are left. Yet they were the most intelligent and economically valuable communities of the old Ottoman Empire. She (Turkey) can hardly aspire to a much higher position than that of a third rate power barely equal in general resources to any of the Balkan states over which she used to rule, and she has herself abdicated the prestige and influence which the possession of the Khalifate had conferred upon her."[*]

But the very learned and accomplished writer, Doctor Buckler, brings out some facts of stupendous importance and significance. To quote his words:

"The range of Anatolian historical monuments and documents covers about five thousand years. The periods represented by remains extend from the third millennium B.C., with its South Cappadocian Cuneiform tablets to the fifteenth century A.D., with its Seljuk architecture and inscriptions. Among the subjects of history on which Anatolian remains throw light are: Law, politics, economics, education, art, (including sculpture) philosophy, literature."

He goes on to say that the term "Anatolia," as here used, covers all of Asia Minor lying west of a line running north from Alexandretta to the Black Sea, and a list of ancient cities and towns having mints of their own in the fourteen classical districts included within that area, works out as follows:

Lycia, Pamphylia and Pisidia	95 towns
Lycaonia, Isauria and Cilicia	82 towns
Phrygia and Galatia	61 towns
Bithynia, Paphlagonia and Pontus	34 towns
Ionia, Lydia and Caria	84 towns
Total	356 towns

Among the sites already excavated, or earmarked for excavation, he mentions Pergamon, Miletus, Sardis, Colophon, Priene, Cnidus; and among those partly spoiled for excavation by their mere existence as modern towns, are Smyrna, Halicarnassus, Adalia, Philadelphia, Thyatira and Ankyra. The last named is now the Turkish capital, Angora. The most, if not all, of the cities mentioned by Doctor Buckler were centers of Greek or Christian culture, or both.

---

[*]   Chirol, *Occident and Orient,* pp. 65–67.

Byron Settlement.

Houses near Athens erected for Asia Minor refugees by the Greek Government.

It is natural that the archeologists, in their anxiety to obtain permission to work in Asia Minor with safety should be very careful to say nothing that might offend the sensibilities of the Turk. They must use all their diplomacy in dealing with him in order that as much as possible may be unearthed of the treasures of Greek art and wisdom that lie buried beneath the land now in the hands of the Khemalists, still wet with the blood of the last survivors of an ancient civilization.

We have then, the following classes who find themselves in the same situation with regard to the Turk, that is to say, who are prevented from saying anything that might offend him: Certain missionaries; the business men with interests still in Turkey; the concession hunters; the diplomats; the archeologists. I believe that many of these are sincere in their admiration of the Turk, founded on the supposition that his crimes have been greatly exaggerated and were more or less justified.

This conviction I do not share and I am convinced that it would have been better for the whole Western world and the Turks as well, if the non-Moslem minorities had been protected, and Christian civilization given a chance to develop in the Ottoman Empire.

As to the great commercial and industrial activity, which Professor Buckler foresaw in 1922, the two following extracts from the press of 1925 are apropos. A writer in a February number of the *Gazetta del Popol,* of Turin, Italy, recently returned from Smyrna, says:

"The appearance of Smyrna is tragic. Even two years and a half after the tragedy the ruins are untouched. For two kilometers along the quay stretch the skeletons—the ghosts of houses. And behind are more miles of streets, lined by other phantom houses, like an endless morgue.

"This phantom city is a terrible symbol of all Turkey. That which above all attracts attention is the disappearance of the Greeks, swept out, extirpated from that city, which was their metropolis in the Levant and where they dominated all forms of activity. The Armenians have also completely disappeared. The Jews endure with difficulty the handicaps which they undergo in their sphere of life.

"The Europeans try to make the best of a bad situation, but those who are not supplied with ample capital, sufficient to allow them to face a thousand daily vexations, which the authorities inflict, are faced with the necessity of themselves retiring.

"All forms of activity in Turkey during the past ages were created by non-Turks. There was nothing of theirs except the army. Ruthlessly the Turks condemn to death all enterprise—commercial and industrial—in which they can not themselves succeed.

"At present Turkey has only three custom houses—Constantinople, Smyrna and Messina. Since the first of January of this year, when the law concerning the customs went into effect, all other ports have been obliged to suspend entirely their traffic. It is not possible for commercial activity to exist in them any more; traffic with Europe has practically ceased entirely. All goods shipped to and from Turkey must be unloaded at one of these towns; go through the vexatious customs formalities, and be reloaded and reshipped to their destinations.[*]

"The rug industry no longer exists. The Armenians and Greeks, who were its personnel, have fled and settled in Rhoades, Piræus, and some at Bari. There no longer remains any one in Smyrna who knows how to make carpets.

"Ten years ago, by the Armenian massacres and deportations, Asia Minor was laid desolate. To-day, the industrious and productive portion of its population has completely disappeared. It will soon become, if not a desert, a wilderness. Everywhere along the coast are cities, which were abandoned to the Turks two years ago and are now completely depopulated. The tillers of the soil have become shepherds and nomads—the land no longer belongs to any one. Within a few years, if God does not work a miracle, and endow the Turks with gifts which they have always lacked, Asia Minor will become a desert in the heart of Mediterranean civilization."

And a writer in a recent number of *Le Temps* of Paris says:

"Constantinople is a dying city. The Bosphorus, once thronged with the world's shipping, is now all but deserted; the offices of

---

This system of concentrating the business of the country at these three places creates the fictitious appearance of increased activity at these ports, at the expense of all the others. Macri, which formerly had fifteen thousand inhabitants, has now a miserable two thousand survivors. The same is also true of Adalia, formerly important, and now completely dead.

foreign business houses are winding up their affairs; the banks will loan money only at the most exorbitant rates. The troubles with the Greeks and Armenians have resulted in the expulsion en masse of those peoples. Even the Turkish population proper is emigrating in the hope of finding brighter commercial prospects."

"As the prosperity of the great city declines, its ancient rivals, Alexandria, Beirut, Saloniki and Piræus are receiving the benefits of its former trade."

How can it be otherwise?

Efficiency to massacre does not mean ability in industry and commerce, and the fanatical destruction of great industrial masses has always proved a serious blow to the prosperity of the country where the crime has occurred, as witness the persecution of the Huguenots in France. In Turkey it has meant ruin.

Chapter 38

ECHOES FROM SMYRNA

As THROWING some light on the spirit in which the foregoing pages have been written, I append the following letters, the first two from American missionary associations, the third from a committee of prominent Turks at Smyrna:

AMERICAN BOARD OF COMMISSIONERS FOR FOREIGN MISSIONS

Incorporated 1812

Congregational House, 14 Beacon Street, Boston, Massachusetts.

March 22, 1923.

Doctor George Horton,

American Consul-General,

Care Consular Bureau, State Dept.,

Washington, D.C.

Dear Doctor Horton,

Enclosed is a letter written by Mr. Getchell in behalf of the missionaries of Smyrna, addressed to Doctor Barton, to have been handed to you on board the steamer which you in some way failed to take.

It was thus delayed and reached my hands only yesterday.

Please accept the sentiments expressed although unfortunately so long delayed in transmission. The original of the letter addressed to Doctor Barton was delivered when the party reached America and was read by him on his return from China.

We are watching events in the Near East with the greatest interest and, as one of the missionaries has said, "with hopes that scarce know themselves from fear".

I have heard that the American Consulate is again functioning in Smyrna and it is possible that you are there once more. If so, it will be a comfort and a relief of many persons whose interests are still largely centered in that city.

I trust that you and your family have maintained your health despite the terrible strain upon you and that you will be able to continue in the splendid cooperation with our missionaries that has characterized your work in the past.

Very sincerely yours,

(Signed) Ernest W. Riggs.

The letter referred to as "enclosed" was as follows:

Athens, Greece,

October 12, 1922.

Reverend James L. Barton, D. D., Secretary of the American Board, 14 Beacon Street, Boston, Mass.

Dear Doctor Barton,

At a recent station meeting of the Smyrna missionaries now refugees in the city of Athens (numbering fourteen adults) a vote was passed recognizing the exceedingly helpful and sympathetic services of our Consul-General, Doctor Horton, during the days of the late Smyrna tragedy. The vote also expressed the desire that a copy of this letter be sent to the State Department, Washington, D.C., and one also to Doctor Horton himself.

During those days of Turkish fire, pillage and massacre, which laid the beautiful city of Smyrna in ashes and rendered homeless her Christian population of not less than 500,000 people, including the refugees from the surrounding towns and villages, Doctor Horton passed through more trying, exacting and dangerous experiences than I could imagine any official of the United States Government, doing service abroad, has ever been called upon to undergo.

Under such circumstances, when our American Consulate was crowded with helpless human beings, all looking to the consul for help and advice, Consul Horton kept cool but never cold.

His warm sympathetic heart went out to each sufferer, and aid was extended wherever possible.

The missionaries are especially grateful for the assistance rendered by Doctor Horton in helping to rescue teachers and pupils from the schools, with the result that not one teacher from the American Girls' Institute, at Smyrna, is missing; and most of the girls, who were in the burning building, have been saved.

Since the flight to Athens, Doctor Horton has been most energetic in helping to feed, clothe and house the needy refugees.

We wish to put on record our appreciation of Doctor Horton's brave and sympathetic efforts for ourselves, as well as the natives of the city.

On behalf of the missionaries of Smyrna Station, I remain,

Very sincerely yours,

(Signed) "Dana K. Getchell."

The third and following letter was received by me in Washington, August 20, 1923, in the Turkish language. Among the signers are Ilimdar Zade Edhiem, President of the Islamic Emigration Committee and Hali Zeki, proprietor of the well-known *Shark Gazette.*

My constant policy during the long time that I was in the Near East, was to befriend, in so far as my official position permitted, all who might be in need of help, irrespective of race or religion.

30 July, 1339 (Turkish date)

Since the appointment of His Excellency, George Horton as Consul-General of the United States in Smyrna, His Excellency has won the heart of the whole Turkish nation by the sympathy and good will, which His Excellency has always shown every Turkish man.

During the Greek occupancy of our country His Excellency, Mr. George Horton, gave full protection and kindly treatment to those of the Turks who went to him for protection and the right of humane existence.

We therefore beg to express our heartiest thanks to His Excellency, Mr. George Horton, for all the interest and kindly services rendered by him for the Turkish nation, which has also created in our hearts a deep and eternal affection for his honorable nation.

(Signed)

Ilimdar Zade Edhem, President of the Islamic Emigration Committee

Sahlebdji Zade Midhat, Merchant

Hussein Djemal, Chemist

Beshir Zade, Merchant

Mehmet Nourri, Carpet Merchant

Hali Zeki, Proprietor of *Shark Gazette*

Hassan Fewzi, Lawyer

Shaih Kadri

Eyyub Sabri, Merchant

Mehmet Emin, Merchant

Mehmet Hamdi, Merchant

Kesreli Hadji Ali, Tobacco Merchant

Berkeli Zade Hadji Bedriddin

Mkr. Ahmet

Kantardji Zade

Mustapha Nouriddin

Mehmet Zeki, Hat Merchant.

Of these and of many other Turks that I have known personally, I have the most friendly and even affectionate recollections. I wish them well and would gladly welcome an occasion that would allow me to be of service to them again.

It is necessary, however, for the honor of the Turkish race that some of its members should denounce the massacres and publicly declare that they are and have always been opposed to them. If the Koran does not advocate the putting to death of the unbeliever as some of its expounders maintain, then it should seem indispensable to the good name of Mohammedanism in general, that all the other Moslems should denounce the Turkish massacres.

The above testimonial was forwarded to me by Mr. Rufus Lane, formerly American consul at Smyrna, who writes among other things:

"I thought it would be a pleasure to you to have as a souvenir of your stay here a few lines from some of your Turkish friends, attesting their sympathy for you.

"One man declares that you saved the lives of his entire family in 1916, by providing them with food, a doctor and a nurse when his mother, his wife and three children were all down with typhus. I know the man well, as also the circumstances, which no doubt you have forgotten."

Chapter 39

CONCLUSION

THE outstanding facts in the preceding narrative are the following:

1. Smyrna was burned by the Turks, as the concluding, at present, act in a consistent policy that has been shaping Moslem history and expansion for centuries, and especially Turkish history since the coming to power of the Young Turks, as displayed in the "Turkifying" murders, tortures and persecutions in Macedonia that led to the First Balkan War (1912); the killing and driving from their homes of the Greeks of Asia Minor during the period just preceding the outbreak of the World War and the destruction of their flourishing villages, (as described by the Frenchman Manciet, writing of the scenes at Phocæa); the deportation of Greeks, men, women and children in the mid-winter of 1916, from the Black Sea region, forcing them to walk in the inclement weather till many thousands perished (as mentioned by Dana K. Getchell, in his letter given above); the doing to death of between eight hundred thousand and a million Armenians in 1915–16; the burning of Smyrna and the massacre of thousands of its inhabitants in 1922.

2. Smyrna was burned by Turkish soldiers at a time when they were in full and complete possession of the city, and the fires were applied first in the Armenian quarter, in which the Turks had been plundering, murdering and raping for several days and where no Armenian was to be found, with the possible exception of such survivors as might be hiding in cellars.

3. Credible non-Greek or non-Armenian witnesses testified to the manner of the burning of Smyrna.

4. A Turkish soldier poured petroleum, or petroleum mixed with gasoline, in the street before the American consular building, causing the fire to be led up to and communicated to the building and endangering the lives of those within.

5. The burning of Smyrna and the massacre and abuse of its Christian inhabitants in the year of our Lord, 1922, was made possible through the mutual jealousies and conflicting commercial

interests of certain Christian powers, and the actual aid, moral and material, furnished by some of them to the Turks.

6. The Turks committed their fearful acts against the Christians and humanity in general in the full conviction that they would meet with no opposition nor even criticism from the United States. They were led to this belief by a loud pro-Turk and anti-Christian propaganda carried on in the American press by certain concession hunters, and other interested writers.

7. No Gladstonian note of horror, protest or revulsion has as yet issued from any official American source, though the Turks have surpassed anything that Gladstone ever dreamed of.

8. The Turks can not regain the confidence and respect of the civilized world until they repent sincerely of their crimes and make all restitution in their power.

9. Concealing such deeds as have been recounted in these chapters or misrepresenting them with the purpose of obtaining material advantages or saving property, reveals a low state of morality, consistent with the spirit of this commercial age.

10. One of the many reasons why Mohammedanism is outstripping Christianity in the latter's ancient birthplace and territory, and in general wherever the two religions meet face to face, is that Christ has been unworthily followed by the people who are sending out the missionaries.

11. Church people in America should become aware of the fact that American missionaries in Turkey can not convert Turks, nor conduct religious exercises at which Turks are present and that the schools in the Ottoman Empire are now being conducted on that basis; and that, if they should convert any Turks, the latter would be killed, and the missionaries and their buildings be in danger of attack.

But the chief lesson of these pages is the growing feebleness of Christianity—divided, insincere, permeated with materialism; undermined and befuddled, in much of its old sturdy and childlike credence, by modern scientific discovery.

Whoever has attended, as I have done at the city of Washington, a general meeting of missionaries, can not have failed to be impressed with the devotion, enthusiasm and spiritual fervor of those noble men and women who carry the beautiful doctrines of Christ to heathen lands. I saw them and heard them soon after my return from the Near East and the Smyrna horror, and I could scarcely refrain from rising to my feet and crying:

"Come home and save us, before it is everlastingly too late!"

APPENDIX

THE fearful and cataclysmic drama of anti-Christ unrolled in these pages is still developing, in all its phases. In the *Christian Advocate* of June 18, 1925, appeared the following editorial, as the leading article, which I quote in full:

A NAME! A NAME!

What's in a name! asks the poet, as if "Nothing" must be the inevitable answer. Yet it is the experience of mankind that the proper answer would be "Everything." For around the name cluster all the qualities of the thing named. The color and scent of the queen of flowers flash out before the imagination at the very name of "rose." So precious are the names of articles of commerce that we find manufacturers of soaps and tooth-pastes, gasolines and lubricants, bread, salves and cigarettes, paying large sums to secure a distinctive name for their special brand, and registering it with the government and defending their sole right to its use with all the authority the laws confer. Shut your eyes and let some one speak the words "Ford" and "Rolls-Royce," and no more ask what's in a name?

There is a Name that is—or must we say was?— above every name. What has happened to it?

A remarkable thing has recently taken place in Turkey. The government called into consultation Asa Kent Jennings, an American resident of Asia Minor (whose name is still borne with honor on the rolls of the Northern New York Conference of the Methodist Episcopal Church). During the war between the Turks and Greeks he had displayed qualities of character, which won him the good opinion of both nations. He was told that the Turkish Republic was seeking to discover some educational method or social agency that would promote the physical, intellectual and moral excellence of the young men and women of the nation. In conference with him a plan was worked out for a system of associations or clubs in large centers, where everything which distinguishes the threefold program of the Young Men's Christian Association shall be put in practice under the official patronage and with the support of the Turkish Government, which is Mohammedan in religion, but under the direction of Mr. Jennings, who is a "Y" secretary and a Methodist preacher. The first of these clubs is to be opened at Angora, the new capital, and the man in charge will be another Methodist preacher, John B. Ascham, of West Ohio, whose illuminating contributions on the European political situation since the war have appeared in these columns from time to time. But it was stipulated by the Angora government these institutions, though redolent of the spirit of Christ, must not bear the name of Christian. That is a fundamental condition. Everything Christian, except the label!

How can this be? The explanation is obvious. From the time of the Crusades, when the wearers of the Cross clashed with the wearers of the Crescent, the name of Christian has been forever tarnished with memories of massacre and war. None of the fruits of the Spirit, the virtues which the Western world likes to connect with the word Christian, come to the mind of the Turk when he sees that name. Thus Christianity, named for the Elder Brother of all mankind, is for a whole nation synonymous with racial and religious enmity.

There are European nations where the name that should be above every name has been dragged in the dust. A London writer who was commissioned to create a Christian literature for the boys of Czechoslovakia proposed to initiate a series of hero-biographies with a life of Jesus Christ. A man who was better acquainted with the people of that country warned him that a life of Christ would kill the series. During the long period of Austrian tyranny over these lands the Church of Rome had so identified itself with the ruling despotism, that everything bearing the Christian name shared the evil reputation of that partnership of oppression and superstition. The Kaiser was gone and the Church disestablished, but a book with the label of Christian would still be viewed with suspicion by the people, as being propaganda for their former masters. Consequently the series will start off with Abraham Lincoln because groups calling themselves Christian have made the name of Christ a reproach.

Mahatma Gandhi of India tells the missionaries that Christ wins him, but Christianity as exemplified by Western political, social and economic standards he does not recognize as a New Testament product. China looks lovingly toward Christ, but becomes suspicious of Christian nations when they are represented by warships, machine guns, and extra-territorial courts, or by predatory foreign business corporations, wringing the last cent from coolie labor at the expense of decency and life itself. "If this is Christ," they say, "let us stick to Confucius !"

Nor is it necessary to go abroad to find the golden name of Christ debased and counterfeited.

The purity of the coinage is entrusted to every one who has named for himself the name of Christ. The excellence of His precepts is sure to be judged by the performance of His professed followers. Many a sermon has failed to convince, convict and convert the sinner, chiefly because the sinner could point to men and women in the congregation whose lives, known and read by their associates, tended to discredit the minister's appeal. Thus, the Name before which every knee should bow commands no homage.

The nation or the individual that takes the name of Christian incurs a weighty responsibility. In some degree the Name of Christ is committed to them. Upon the manner in which that person, church, society, or nation discharges its responsibility will measurably depend the esteem which others will give to that Name.

I have read this editorial time and time again, and all that I can get from it is that the name of Christ, of a soap, of a tooth-paste, of a salve, of a grease, of a cigarette, should be used as long as it produces results, but when no longer potent, should be dropped. This is certainly what has been officially done in Turkey with the Name. What the church people of America should understand is that Mohammedanism is marching on with firebrand and scimitar, the greatest enemy of Christianity in the world, and that dropping the Name of Christ and the teaching of the Master, by great Christain organizations, is another victory for the Prophet. No sophistry, however ingenious, can obscure this fact.

Let us hope that this move on their part is the prelude to a great awakening and revulsion on the part of Western Christians:

And as Peter was beneath in the palace, there cometh one of the maids of the high priest.

And when she saw Peter warming himself, she looked upon him, and said, And thou also wast with Jesus of Nazareth.

But he denied, saying, I know not, neither understand I what thou sayest. And he went out into the porch; and the cock crew.

But Peter afterward testified in quite a different manner. There can be no working for Christ in any place where his Name is dropped. That concession is in itself a victory for the Powers of darkness.

In the press of October 25, 1925, appeared an article by George Seldes, describing the persecution of the Christian Chaldeans, on the Turkish-British frontier, near Mosul. It was announced as the first of a series, but the other articles have not been published. It is so similar to the other well-authenticated happenings of a like nature described in the foregoing pages, that it forms a logical continuation of the narrative. I quote from the *Washington Post* of October 25, 1925:

Mosul, Mesopotamia, October 18 (By Mail to Cairo).—In a beautiful village oasis called Zakho, on the British-Turkish frontier in the biblical country, amidst peaceful surroundings, I found witnesses to-day to a terrible tragedy which Mohammedan Arabs as well as Christians asked me to relate to the Christian world.

It is the story of the deportation of eight thousand Chaldean Christians from the frontier, of their march into the interior of Turkey, of how the Turks murdered men, violated women and threw infants over precipices. It is a story of suffering unparalleled in recent times and every word here written is sworn to on the Bible by chieftains of villages and their priests and attested by Archbishop Timothy, their spiritual father.

OLD AND ILL SLAIN

"Will the Christian world believe that such things can happen now!" asked Archbishop Timothy as the Mukhtar—or sheif—of Murga, knelt and told his story. What the Mukhtar told in Arabic was this:"

"As God is my witness and by the blood of Christ I swear that on the march north the Turks killed five men who, on account of their age, could not keep up with the procession. Three women who were ill they stoned to death. On the first night we camped near a fountain. The Turkish officers and soldiers put out the lights and seized all the young pretty girls and carried them to the fields. All night we heard the screams and cries of the girls and women. They clouded the skies with their mournful cries and it was like the Day of Judgment.

"On the third day one of the women was in the pangs of childbirth. The Turks waited until the baby was born. Other women took the baby, but the mother was too feeble to march, so she was shot. At the Ozozan Mountains three men and two women who tried to escape were shot to death. Their young orphaned children were then killed."

This statement, in colder official form, I saw later in records sworn to and attested by the British governor of Mesopotamia.

A letter has just been received by me (October, 1925) from Doctor George E. White, President of the ill-fated missionary college at Marsovan, Turkey. This important and once flourishing institution has been reopened at Saloniki, Greece. I quote the following from its circular:

"The refugee peoples of the Near East deserve all the sympathy they receive from American friends. This tragic "movement of populations" is the greatest of its kind in all history. There are 160,000 refugees in the city of Saloniki, 800,000 in the province of Macedonia, and 1,500,000 in the whole of Greece. . . . The Greek Government has revised its laws for the express purpose of welcoming American education. . . . Saloniki is building mightily at the present time; it is the point where the Greek seaman from the South meets the Slav plowman from the North; Moslem Jew and Christian have felt at home for many generations; Saloniki is moving forward under a Christian government reestablished in 1912, after alien domination since 1430."

Let us hope that this Christian college will "build mightily" in its new habitat, where it has a great and sacred mission: so to diffuse the spirit of the Master through the Balkans that race hatreds will diminish in those regions, wars cease, and the remnants of the glorious old Byzantine Empire will be able to reestablish that Christian civilization, which the Turk has driven out of Asia Minor. Or, if that is too much, let us at least hope that the influence of its teachings may be sufficiently great to prevent any of the Balkan States from joining with the Moslems or the Bolsheviks to destroy their neighbors.

INDEX

FURTHER READINGS FROM STERNDALE CLASSICS

Ottoman Empire and WWI
Lewis Einstein, *Inside Constantinople.*
George Hornton, *The Blight of Asia.*
Grace Knapp, *The Tragedy of Bitlis.*
Henry Morgenthau, *Ambassador Morgenthau's Story.*
Rafael de Nogales, *Four Years Beneath the Crescent.*
Harry Stuermer, *Two War Years in Constantinople.*
Clarence Ussher, *An American Physician in Turkey.*

Ottoman Empire and Provinces
George Hamilton, *Through Armenia on Horseback.*
Robert Curzon, *Armenia: A Year in Erzeroom.*
W. J. Childs, *Across Asia Minor on Foot.*
William Ramsay, *Impressions of Turkey.*

Ottoman Empire and the Eastern Question
Duke of Argyll, *Our Responsibilities for Turkey.*